Ewa Hryniewicz-Yarbrough from Poland in 1984, bring .... of life under a totalitarian regime, where the personal was always political. In essay after essay in *Objects of Affection*, her remarkable debut, Hryniewicz-Yarbrough shows the immigrant's double perspective, exploring a "bi-polar" world of displacement and rootlessness, geography and memory, individual and family history, always with an acute awareness of losses and gains that accompany adaptation to a new language and culture and the creation of a new identity.

★

"Ewa Hryniewicz-Yarbrough uses the phrase 'alien intonations' to describe one way that cultures and castes recognize outsiders. She is as astute about these markers as she is about all facets of the immigrant experience. These essays view Poland, her first world, with an unillusioned nostalgia, while viewing America—here is another oxymoron—as a vast material vale of soul-making. *Objects of Affection* is smart and deeply heartfelt, which is mercifully *not* an oxymoron."

> – SVEN BIRKERTS, author of *Changing the Subject: Art and Attention in the Internet Age*

"Ewa Hryniewicz-Yarbrough's *Objects of Affection* is exquisite. Compact, powerful, and insightful, her essays accrue to an arresting thinker's spiritual and intellectual autobiography that illuminates, in a glib and divisive era, the complex experience of immigration, taking up questions of language, culture, memory, identity, and history with eloquence and an alertness to those moments when our common humanity shines through. These are essays to savor."

> – RICHARD HOFFMAN, author of *Half the House: A Memoir* and *Love & Fury*

"'We live much more in a language than in a country,'" Ewa Hryniewicz-Yarbrough, essayist and translator, writes in her stunning first collection, *Objects of Affection*. 'Places are both physical and metaphysical,' and 'only things that vanish stay forever the same' in memory. There is wisdom and sweet pathos in these nineteen exquisitely wrought meditations, but above all, I felt happy reading them, guided by a sure-handed writer through the 'messy materiality' of existence, first in her early years on the 'wrong side' of the Iron Curtain, then in a new equally compelling life in an America not yet 'choked by politics.' I longed to stay with her words and in her worlds."

– MEGAN MARSHALL, Pulitzer Prize-winning author of *Margaret Fuller: A New American Life* and *Elizabeth Bishop: A Miracle for Breakfast*

"In Ewa Hryniewicz-Yarbrough's thought-provoking collection of essays, *Objects of Affection*, the writer and translator reflects on the before and after of an immigrant/émigré: is one's life halved or doubled at the border? She reminds us that to adopt a language is to take nothing, not even its clichés, for granted. Hryniewicz-Yarbrough comes to see her life between two cultures as being like the art of translation itself—a rich mixture of loss and serendipity, frustration and discovery, where you try to carry across what is most precious, where every word is a choice, and hard won."

– A. E. STALLINGS, translator and poet, author of *Olives*

"Ewa Hryniewicz-Yarbrough's *Objects of Affection* is an astonishing debut. Her essays range across an amazing number of subjects – language, family, love, loss, reading, war, possessions, tea, hair, letter-writing—and yet the collection feels always of a piece because each essay is the story of her mind thinking about its own object of affection. And she thinks in probing, honest, and crystalline language. The sentences are beautiful. It is now, I think, commonly accepted that the essay in America has undergone a renaissance since the 1980s. What this wonderful, cosmopolitan book, born as it is of immigration and wide experience, reminds us is that the essay has always had the capacity to be global in its reach and sympathies. I admire Hryniewicz-Yarbrough and this book very much."

"This book is a wonderful contribution to a debate that we hear these days, a conversation concerning joys and curses of living in a multilingual world. Ewa Hryniewicz-Yarbrough discusses her life between Polish and English, between her childhood in a town in Poland and her mature years in California and New England, between two literatures . . . But there's also a third language here, her own way of speaking, her quiet, modest, intelligent, convincing voice."

Objects of Affection

OBJECTS OF AFFECTION

Essays
by
Ewa Hryniewicz-Yarbrough

BRADDOCK AVENUE BOOKS

UNCOMMON BOOKS · UNCOMMON READERS

Printed in the United States of America
10 9 8 7 6 5 4 3 2 1

FIRST EDITION, February 2018

ISBN 10: 0-9989667-3-1
ISBN 13: 978-0-9989667-3-1

Some of the essays in this collection have appeared in slightly different versions in the following publications:
"The Bearable Lightness of Being" in *The American Scholar*
"Reading Under the Table" in *The Threepenny Review*
"In Zbigniew Herbert's Garden" in *The Threepenny Review*
"Europa, Europa" in *Agni*
"My War Zone" in *The Missouri Review*
"Objects of Affection" in *Ploughshares* and *Best American Essays 2012*
"Our Daily Drink" in *The Normal School*
"Bottom , Thou Art Translated" in *TriQuarterly*
"The Politics of Hair" in *EuropeNow*
"Mad Menards" in *The Threepenny Review*
"A Non-Sentimental Journey" in *Agni Online*
"Little Bowls of Colors" in *The American Scholar*

Cover design by Maria Gromek
Interior design by Savannah Adams

Alleyway Books
an imprint of
Braddock Avenue Books
P.O. Box 502
Braddock, PA 15104

www.braddockavenuebooks.com

Braddock Avenue Books is distributed by Small Press Distribution.

For Steve, Tosia, and Lena

contents

OBJECTS OF AFFECTION

essays

was it worth coming and going, was it—
yes no yes no
erase nothing

—Adam Zagajewski, "Was it"

THE BEARABLE
LIGHTNESS OF BEING

In 2009 my husband got a teaching job in Boston. It wouldn't start until September, so that gave us plenty of time to do the things people do when they know they'll be moving. In mid-March we put our house up for sale, hoping we'd find a buyer before the beginning of the fall semester. The day after it was listed, we had three offers. We were overjoyed that in such a terrible real-estate market we'd be able to sell but dismayed it had happened so fast, since we had to stay in Fresno until the school year ended. The simplest thing to do, we decided, was to sell the house and then rent it from its new owners for a few weeks.

I dreaded the moment when I'd walk out the front door for the last time, weepy and emotional. That was what happened in the summer of 1985 when I returned from the US for a short visit to Wrocław, a city in southwest Poland, where I attended college and lived for thirteen years. At that time I had no clue under what circumstances I'd ever return to Poland. After the brutal suppression of Solidarity and the nightmare of martial law, no one would venture optimistic predictions about the demise of communism in that part of the world. It was quite possible I'd never again see the house I lived in. As my uncle was driving me to the airport and we reached the end of my street, I looked back one more time. I wanted to return to America to join the man I was in love with, whom I'd met in Virginia on an academic exchange program the previous year, but I was also heartbroken and grieving for the loss of my home. The only place I'd ever left before was my hometown in northeastern Poland; that, though, was a different departure. I'd outgrown it and was overjoyed at the prospect of going to college in a big city. I knew I'd miss the landscape of my childhood, the woods I explored with friends, and the lakes in which I swam each summer. I also knew that I could always hop on a train and go there. After all, as my grandmother said to my mother and father who were ill at ease at my moving so far away, I wasn't leaving for another country.

I had every reason to believe that I would experience some degree of sadness when we were driving away from Fresno, but nothing like that happened. I was as detached as if I were watching someone else. When we reached the freeway and the city gradually receded into a blurry background, both the house and the place itself stopped existing—they vanished from my consciousness.

Was I surprised at my reaction? Yes and no. I loved our home with its light modern design, its floor-to-ceiling windows, the irregularly shaped back yard, and the eye of a pool surrounded by boulders and redwoods. It was the space that over the years had become my refuge, the way houses are supposed to be. But I never learned to like the city it was in, even though I lived there twenty-one years, much longer than anywhere else. Not that I didn't try.

Before we moved to Fresno we'd lived in rented apartments and houses in two very different but attractive university towns. Those were the first years after I came to the United States, and back then I still felt like a tourist, someone for whom everything is new, riveting, and at the same time provisional. Since the two towns would be only small dots on the map of my life, I never tried to form an attachment to them.

By the time we moved to California, we already had a baby. Children tend to awaken nesting instincts even in those devoted to nomadic life. And children of immigrants bear an even more serious responsibility. They're supposed to give these uprooted people a sense of rootedness and belonging. After our daughter was born, I suddenly felt settled in America, no longer sitting on the fence, to use the clichéd metaphor. I still kept looking over it, something most immigrants do, but I felt more connected to my adopted country. I just needed a tangible place, a house, a city, the space and area I would make my home.

Fresno had been uncharted territory for me. I understood that it lay in the Central Valley, flanked to the east by the Sierra Nevada range. That was the extent of my knowledge, enough to trigger fanciful imaginings. The names *Valley* and *Sierra Nevada* conjured images of lush green vegetation, crystalline brooks, majestic mountains. The images were kitschy, yet I went there believing they would somehow prove true. When we drove into the town on a sultry August day, I was already disappointed. We'd entered the Valley a few hours earlier, and it wasn't at all what I had envisioned. The fields on both sides of the freeway looked parched, the vegetation was the color of copper, and the mountains were nowhere to be seen because a thick cloud of pollution enveloped the area. We endured what remained of a hellish summer with temperatures hovering around 110 degrees, which, as we later found out, was the norm. Despite those setbacks, I hoped that with time I'd grow to like the place and be able to consider it home. I kept telling myself what the city's longtime residents often said: Fresno may not be appealing, but it's close to great places. We could get to Yosemite or Sequoia National Park within an hour and a half, to the ocean in two and a half hours.

After about two years, I realized I'd never feel at home there. Our house was a comfortable oasis, but the at-home feeling didn't continue farther than the back yard. I was familiar with the city; I drove in it every day, had friends and a job, yet on some level it continued to be alien, not mine. For the first few years I felt my foreignness most acutely. Whenever we returned from our travels, I didn't experience what one is supposed to experience on returning home. I never felt affected like I did when I went back to Poland. I often asked myself whether the overall unattractiveness of the area could account for my sense of homelessness. Would I have felt differently if the place had been more appealing? Aesthetics may have played some role but liking a place doesn't translate into feeling at home. Could it have been the landscape and the climate which were so different from those of my childhood? Was I searching for something that I simply couldn't have, that simply didn't exist?

*

We're all born into our childhood homes by happenstance since we don't choose the place of our birth. Yet those places, familiar like no others, determine our identity and create the parameters of what we will always search for in a home. A friend once told me that her Irish family had settled on Long Island and had always lived there. When she went to Ireland for the first time, she realized why Long Island had become their chosen place. "I could see," she said, "that they were looking for the landscape that would remind them of home, and they found an area that with its greenery and proximity to water resembled somewhat what they had left behind."

For my father, who was born in Lithuania, the standard of natural beauty was always the scenery he remembered from his childhood. Each time we went for a walk outside the town we lived in, he would point to a clump of birch trees, inhale the smell of wet soil wafting from the meadows, and say, "Just like back home." He'd lost his birthplace after the Yalta Conference, when his native region was incorporated into the Soviet Union. His family was Polish, so they decided to join thousands of other "repatriates" and re-settle in the region in Poland that the communist newspeak labeled "the Recovered Territories." He wasn't a typical exile as he never had to learn another language and culture, yet every so often he grew nostalgic for his childhood landscape.

Sometimes when life forces immigrants to settle in places that don't resemble the ones they have left behind, they attempt to tame those strange surroundings by giving them names that can conjure up their old country. It's enough to look at the American map to detect names such as Frankfurt, Paris, Moscow, Prague, and Warsaw within geographic longitudes that have nothing in common with the ur-places they refer to. The naming is the outward part of the exiles' domesticating scheme. In their homes they hold on to odds and ends they have brought with them: a frayed and faded wall hanging, a picture of their patron saint, a chipped plate, a photograph album. I've seen homes whose owners have been adding over the years to this trove of objects. Paintings of landscapes, folk-art sculptures, rugs, bedspreads, vases—the familiar props that are supposed to create the illusion of home and subdue the foreignness of the environment.

*

People who have always lived in the country of their birth, even if they move away from the place where they were born, remain ensconced in the cocoon of their own language and culture. They don't need instructions on how to apply for a driver's license or enroll their children in school. They know that a drugstore houses a pharmacy and that a postman will pick up their outgoing letters from the mailbox. They recognize the elements of their environment, shop in stores that look like the ones they remember from before their move, watch reruns of the TV shows they watched as children, follow the fortunes of their favorite sports teams. They may feel like exiles from their childhood—who doesn't—but in all likelihood that's the only exile they'll ever know. Their lives are relatively seamless and rarely divided into *before* and *after*.

People who have been forced to leave their homeland or who have left it by choice experience their lives as fragmented. Though their new reality may be attractive and even fascinating, they view it from a distance. The election of a politician they despise may irritate them, but it's an abstract irritation, somewhat lighter than what they would have felt back at home. The reality they inhabit seems remote and causes them little pain or excitement. The poet Czesław Miłosz, whose own life was marked by displacement, captured that state of mind very well when he said that an immigrant, "locked in his misanthrope's castle," interacts with the natives in a superficial manner. And when he has learned to understand what is being said around him, he will always hear alien intonations. After living in the United States for more than thirty years, Miłosz decided to return to Poland, where he could feel at home at last.

The notion of "alien intonations" works the other way as well. The immigrant's own intonations mark him forever as alien. Most immigrants sooner or later learn the language of their new country because they know how vital language is to the at-home feeling. They can express themselves comfortably in it, but it can never quite replace the language which they learned as children by osmosis and which they grasp intuitively. Being cut off from one's language is hard, and there's no question that it exacerbates the feeling of homelessness. It's hardest, however, for writers. They can't help but be painfully aware of how the day-to-day living in another language makes the mother tongue slowly erode and pale, and how much effort it takes to keep it alive. In *Speak, Memory* Nabokov admits his "fear of losing or corrupting, through alien influence, the only thing [he] had salvaged from Russia—her language." Many writers continue to write in their native language even when they know that their words may not reach the audience back home. They hold on to the native tongue since in their otherwise homeless state it is the only home they'll ever have. Some writers can't cope with the separation and grow silent. Others, however—maybe the ones with greater linguistic aptitude—try to make a life for themselves in the language of their new country. Nabokov, Joseph Conrad, Samuel Beckett, Milan Kundera, and Ha Jin are just a few of those who gained recognition for the works they wrote in what was at one point a foreign language. Nabokov, Beckett, and Kundera each wrote in his own language before deciding to switch to English or French. Conrad and Ha Jin began to write fiction in English, having never done so in their native language.

Conrad, like Nabokov, was fluent in French which was the language the Russian and Polish landed gentry spoke. But unlike Nabokov, who had English governesses and learned English as a child, Conrad initially knew only six English words. By the time his first book, *Almayer's Folly*, was published, he had not only mastered English but also developed his highly distinctive and hauntingly evocative style. In 1919 he wrote a short author's note to a new edition of *A Personal Record*, a book of reminiscence on his early life. The note addresses the question of his writing in English—a question that every writer who works in an acquired language feels bound to consider sooner or later. Because reviews and critical articles often discussed Conrad's "choice" of English, he wanted to correct that misconception. He had no choice in the matter, he noted. It was the genius of the language that adopted him and let him discover his natural gift for writing in English. If this seems like too optimistic a picture, we need to keep in mind that Conrad wrote those words when he was at the peak of his career, an admired and acclaimed novelist. By that time, English must have felt natural to him. He goes on to say what many emigrant writers often say: if he hadn't turned to English, he wouldn't have become a writer. I'm not sure if that statement can be taken at face value. It's not only the lure of the language that accounts for Conrad's and others' decisions. Without the splinter of exile, they might not have turned to the solace of writing. But dwelling on the experience of disorientation, estrangement, homelessness—those permanent fixtures in an immigrant's life—is pointless. It's better to talk about the redemption or even triumph afforded by what was at first a foreign language, particularly when one is addressing one's newly acquired audience.

Do writers like Conrad or Kundera feel that the language they write in is theirs the way their mother tongue is? Most likely not, if only because they have a double perspective and see the new language through the prism of their original tongue. A Polish short-story writer and essayist Gustaw Herling-Grudziński, who lived in Italy and wrote all his literary works in Polish, once said that when he wrote in Italian, he felt as if he were touching that language with a thick glove. When he wrote in his mother tongue, he felt it "with the thin and innervated skin of [his] bare hands." This metaphor perfectly conveys how some writers perceive their adopted language.

But for most writers, writing in another language is exhilarating. Though they may worry, as Nabokov did, that their English prose will never attain the level of the one written in their native tongue, that doesn't keep them from embracing it. They love the resistance of the new language, the discovery that comes with it, the discipline it demands. They turn each word and phrase over many times, savoring it like a morsel of delicious if somewhat mysterious food. Their home in a new language may never have all the intimacies and comforts of the old home, but it's a home just the same.

English has become such a home for me, too. When I came to the United States, I was in the comfortable position of knowing the language, since I had an MA in English literature and had been reading books in English for many years. My English at the time was the English I had learned reading Jane Austen, Henry James, and James Joyce, and it had little to do with the living language I heard every day. While I was fine writing papers and often drew praise from my professors, I was aware that I sounded formal and therefore distant in casual social exchanges. Now and then I had the eerie feeling that the person speaking English wasn't really me, that it was a badly translated version of myself, and that I was playing a scripted role in which the words I used were unable to confront my true self. I even wondered if my husband knew the real me.

Gradually, as I used English at home all the time, I grew comfortable with it and gave up my metaphysical musings. I was in love with my adopted language, elated and obsessed, as if I'd again fallen for a person I used to know but had underestimated and he'd just returned from a 10-year sojourn abroad.

To test my newly acquired linguistic confidence, I decided to try my hand at translating a Polish novel, *Annihilation* by Piotr Szewc. After it was published, I slowly moved into translating poetry. As English dominated my daily life, like Nabokov I began to worry about my Polish losing its vigor. To prevent it, I started a journal in my native language. A few years later, I decided to keep one in English. I wanted to write in my adopted language as well. In English I wrote about books I'd been reading, whereas I wrote more personal entries in Polish, as if English were still a more public language for me. If anyone requires proof of how schizophrenic an immigrant's existence can be, this is it.

In 2006, my fear that I would lose my native tongue led to a decision to translate Philip Levine's poems into Polish. That year I wrote the last entry in my English-language journal. I still keep the other one and have noticed that increasingly the Polish entries are interspersed with the English ones. I have stopped evading my private life when I write in English, and the internal division is gone.

Some years ago, in Kraków, I attended a J. M. Coetzee reading. He read in English from his novel *Slow Man*. I sat close to an open door through which I could hear the simultaneous Polish translation. I was having a hard time focusing on his words. Gradually, my hearing adapted and I managed to follow the novel, though I had to continue making an effort to block out the sounds of Polish. At that moment I had an epiphany: this is my life.

*

We have now lived for some time in a small town north of Boston. The surroundings have an air of familiarity that Fresno never had. The vegetation is very much like the vegetation in Poland and so is the climate. The first blizzard here transported me back to my childhood when winters in northeast Poland were snowy and unrelenting. The smaller scale of things also reminds me of the place I come from. The preponderance of sloping roofs as well as many church steeples adds to the sense of the familiar. Why, then, isn't my feeling of homelessness gone?

It would be easy to say that I'm one of those immigrants who feel alienated in their new country no matter the situation. Easy but incorrect. The sense of estrangement, a given in an immigrant's life, doesn't necessarily convert into misery and unhappiness. My life feels full and satisfactory, and I'm not unhappy. I follow the political and cultural events here. I have friends, American and Polish. I do try to stay abreast of the Polish scene, now and then cook Polish food, and visit Poland every year. I don't wallow in nostalgia and pine for Poland, weeping into my borscht on Christmas Eve. I'm well adapted, assimilated, yet the feeling that this isn't mine persists. It sometimes surfaces during exchanges with others. I become aware of the gap separating us when I am unable to follow the conversation. Even though I share a lot of cultural references with my fellow Americans, there are many I'm not familiar with. I didn't play the same back-yard games, tell the same jokes, or hum the same songs. I witnessed different events from the ones they did, or if the events were the same, we viewed them from different perspectives. We were told different stories by our parents and grandparents. Our collective memory and our dreams are different. I didn't live under the Nazi occupation, but to this day I occasionally have dreams in which I'm being chased by the Nazis or hiding from the Gestapo.

The same dates provoke dissimilar associations. If I say "Remember how things were in 1968?" my American friends will most likely think of campus unrest and the assassinations of Martin Luther King Jr. and Bobby Kennedy, while I'll think of the anti-Semitic hysteria provoked and fanned by Poland's communist party. I'll also think of the Prague Spring and its aftermath—the Warsaw Pact invasion of Czechoslovakia. I'm aware of those gaps even with my husband of thirty years. I sometimes have to remind him that we were raised in different cultural environments and that I can't identify certain names, facts, and allusions. Do I feel bothered by that? I must say I don't. Does it contribute to my feeling of homelessness? Possibly so.

If someone asks where home is, to spare them a lengthy explanation, I'll say that America is home, as if I could readily claim the whole country but not a specific town or community. Maybe it's easier to feel at home on a macro than a micro scale. The local, if it is ever to be transformed into a place we call home, requires a sense of mine-ness. Still, even in this new more congenial environment, I don't experience it beyond my physical home.

Poland, where I haven't lived for thirty-three years, has undergone many changes since my emigration. I've had to re-learn plenty—from political parties to stores' return policies—but my native country hasn't lost its familiarity. I can still recall and recognize its sights, smells, sounds. I can name the trees and the weeds, the birds and the bugs, and find shortcuts in places I haven't been before. Despite all this, the feeling of homelessness besets me there too. My own sense of belonging and others' perceptions of me have changed. I'm no longer included, no longer part of "we." Friends and family members often remind me of my outsider position when they address me as "you in America." They cannot know that once I return to the United States, this "you" doesn't change to "we," that I don't metamorphose into an insider, even though outwardly I'm included. I pay taxes, vote, and have the same rights as everybody else. When I get together with my immigrant friends, all of whom have American citizenship, this exclusion—this time in reverse—continues as neither they nor I include fellow Americans in the first-person plural.

Should someone wonder about my ethnic origin, my accent will dispel any doubts as it loudly announces that I don't belong here like those who were born here. Naturalization's magic works only so far. I have the right to express myself freely, but I have to practice the kind of caution that most natives would find crippling. Even when I am among people who just a few minutes ago were slamming the excesses of America's corporate power, I don't feel free to make negative comments about some absurdity of local public life, denounce the vacuity of popular culture, or mock the widespread gut-level approach to elections. I can only speak my mind among intimate friends. Even with America's openness to outsiders, I am perceived as a guest: a guest of long standing, but someone who nevertheless should be on her best behavior. Guests by definition aren't at home. In Poland it's still okay for me to castigate boorish and corrupt politicians, complain about the pathetic state of health care, or bash the political ambitions of the church. But there people assume I'm out of the loop. I live abroad, so how much can I know much about Poland's reality? I'm automatically relegated to the role of a foreigner and silenced. If I were to return, I know I'd soon be treated like everybody else, though it would take me a long time to learn to fit in. Or I might never be able to. I see, feel, think differently now. My perspective has changed. My compatriots and I would speak the same language, but our vocabulary wouldn't be the same.

Wherever I am, I'm constantly reminded of the caesura that appeared in my life when I immigrated. In America my life *before* doesn't exist. I have no past—as if I had been born only after I arrived here. Few people show interest in my previous life. Poland hasn't been a major player in world politics, so maybe its minor role on the world stage could account for this lack of interest. But my foreign friends who come from places that are principal players have the same experience. It's not that Americans are provincial and self-centered or that the country is so big. This lack of interest is only natural. People everywhere, even in places with claims to cosmopolitanism, live in the here and now, and are interested in what pertains directly to their lives. When I visit Poland, the situation repeats itself. No one seems very interested in my life in America. I feel like Irena, a character in Kundera's novel *Ignorance*, who on a visit to Prague invites her old friends to a restaurant hoping to revive their friendship. She would like to tell them about her life in France, but they only want to talk about their own concerns. She feels that through their lack of interest in her life abroad "they amputated 20 years from her life." In the same way, my life can be said to have been cut short both in Poland and in America.

Yet I don't feel incomplete. Quite the contrary. I feel some- times as though I'd been given a gift of two lives. I draw suste- nance from two cultures, read books in Polish and English, write and translate in both languages. And while I'm fine with that situation, others' perceptions attempt to mold my image to their expectations. A few years ago during our stay in Poland, my sister was telling me that a mutual Polish friend who lives in Germany had become "very German." I said I hadn't noticed. After this exchange I turned to my younger daughter and asked her how she saw me. "Oh, you're definitely Polish," she said. To her, a young American, I'm just as Polish as I am to other Americans, who sometimes—out of well- meant but ill-considered courtesy—call me Polish-American. They have no way of knowing that I don't feel hyphenated. People in Poland, on the other hand, proclaim that they see an American in me, even if they'd be unable to say what makes me American. I seem different, as anyone who's been away for a long time must seem, and their way of dealing with that is to replace the real me with a cluster of stereotypical national characteristics. I don't have two different identities that I turn on and off depending on where I am. I am the same person here and over there, but as an outsider in my native country, I tend to provoke simplistic generalizations.

I've learned to cherish my outsider status, that bosom friend of homelessness. I won't maintain, though, that homelessness is a desirable state. What sane person would want to be homeless if she had a choice? Home is something we all long for, no matter our personal histories and backgrounds. But homelessness can also bestow unexpected benefits. It gives me the kind of freedom that I wouldn't have otherwise. I don't feel boxed in by national boundaries, don't feel beholden to a sense of communality or collectivity, or compelled to follow the accepted cultural obligations. With no pressure to be loyal to any particular group, it's easier for me to avoid engaging in group think. I never liked being swept up in national euphoria or mourning. I remember my discomfort during the heady days of Solidarity in Poland when unwavering allegiance to the nascent movement was the order of the day and criticism of any kind was treated like betrayal. Being homeless, I'm less likely to succumb to the pull of national orthodoxies, Polish and American alike, which, like any orthodoxies, stifle independent thinking. I still have Polish attachments, affections, predilections, but I hope I've discarded the unwieldy baggage of ethnicity and nationalism, and escaped the narrow and often constricting local perspective.

*

Today more and more people experience the state of homelessness. It's no longer reserved for immigrants, exiles, victims of history or fate. It's a feature of modern life, a result of globalization, of the world's greater uniformity. When I left Poland, America seemed like another planet. To young Poles today it's not so. Mass media are the same all over the world. We watch the same shows and movies, hear the same news, the same ads assault us everywhere. In Paris, Prague, Budapest, New York, or Calcutta, we can watch the Academy Awards or the Super Bowl on TV, eat Chinese takeout, buy a T-shirt made in Indonesia or earrings from Morocco. English has become the modern lingua franca, and communication is possible, no matter where we are. This trend toward global uniformity should make it easier for us to feel at home, since the world has become more predictable and recognizable. Even though we may feel comfortable and at home, paradoxically, we also feel homeless. When more and more of the world becomes the same, we lose our underpinning and our sense of rooted-ness. It's difficult to feel at home in a world that has suddenly become too big, but today the feeling of homelessness isn't as acute as the feeling earlier generations of immigrants or exiles experienced.

Jean Améry is the adopted name of Hans Mayer, a Jewish writer born in Austria. A survivor of Auschwitz, Buchenwald, and Bergen-Belsen, he changed his German name as a sign of radical separation from his birthplace and his rejection of German culture, though he continued to write in German. For many years after the war he refused to visit Germany. He had no choice but to be an exile. He always experienced a profound sense of loss which he summed up in his own words: "Home is the land of one's childhood and youth. Whoever has lost it remains lost himself, even if he has learned not to stumble about in the foreign country as if he were drunk." I lost the land of my childhood and youth, but I don't feel that I have lost myself. In the tally of my life's losses and gains, the gains are more numerous.

READING UNDER THE TABLE

I don't remember when exactly I learned to read, but my father used to tell me that one day I picked up the newspaper while he was taking an after-dinner nap, and when he woke he saw me perusing the front page. He asked me jokingly to read something to him, and I did, surprising him with my unexpected fluency. He had seen me poring over children's books before, and both he and my mother often read to me, pointing out individual letters and words, but no one had ever sat down to teach me how to transform the black marks on the page into meaningful sounds—yet there I was reading a news story. Since my recollections are limited, I can't be sure whether my father's anecdote was true or apocryphal. I do remember, though, that I knew how to read when I entered first grade. Initially my teacher, Mrs. M., was mildly annoyed that I was so far ahead of the rest, but she soon put my ability to good use.

She was pregnant at the time and needed to visit the bathroom quite often, so she'd make me sit in front of the class and read out loud. I enjoyed being in the limelight and playing teacher. It beat reading to my doll and one-eyed teddy bear.

Back then in Poland when a student passed to another grade with all A's (which were actually all 5's), he or she received a book at the end of the school year as an award. These books were always at a typical student's reading level, and each teacher picked them out at a bookstore for her high-achieving charges. I remember that my first year I got a lovely chapter book by Maria Konopnicka titled *The Story of the Dwarves and Orphan Marysia*. My teacher knew I needed a book that would provide many hours of reading. This one had magnificent illustrations by Jan Marcin Szancer that I was mesmerized by. When I passed to third grade, in recognition of my achievement my teacher handed me *The Seven Watches of the Gravedigger Joachim Rybka* by Gustaw Morcinek. While the year before I knew the author of the book I received—we read her poems in class—the name of my new book's writer told me nothing. I went home, proudly showed my certificate to admiring family members, then lay down on the couch doing what I usually did—reading.

I must have left the book lying somewhere instead of putting it on the shelf, and my mother picked it up. She knew who Morcinek was. She was familiar with some of his short stories. When she opened *The Seven Watches*, she saw the school's inscription with the date and the teacher's and the principal's signatures. She began reading and very quickly realized it wasn't suitable for an eight-year old. It had folksy humor and many bawdy scenes. She told my father about it, and they both thought the whole incident was funny. Not for a moment did they worry that the book could have destroyed my nascent moral sense. They figured that my teacher was familiar with Morcinek as the author of some children's books and had just assumed that this was one of them. Since my mom knew the principal, she carried the book to her, not to complain but to share what she considered a hilarious incident. The principal read the novel and returned it to my mother but the page with the inscription was gone. Even though my parents would have never done anything with it except use it as a subject of an amusing anecdote, the administrator must have decided that it was better to spare the school any possible future embarrassment. *The Seven Watches* ended up on a bookshelf, and we never revisited the subject.

Since both my parents worked, I went home to an empty apartment when I got out of school before 11 or 12. I was afraid to light the stove, so I made myself a cup of cold tea, adding a lot of sugar to it to compensate for its unnatural temperature, and ate a sandwich that my mother had left for me before she went to work. After I dumped my school bag on my desk, one of many items left behind by Germans fleeing from the Red Army, I went to my parents' room, which also served as our living and dining area.

There against the wall, facing the kitchen door, stood a large and strange piece of furniture whose undisputed virtue was versatility. It combined wardrobe, cupboard, and even a fold-down escritoire. On each side it had a narrow closet where my parents kept their clothes: the right one was my mother's, the left one my father's. Between the closets this construction had two shelves behind glass where we kept a few mismatched "better" porcelain cups, dessert plates, a small vase, and the figurine of a dancer with one of her ballet shoes broken off. Right underneath was the folding leaf with a lock in the middle and a key that was never turned. This was the place for important documents, a bottle of vodka for unexpected guests, and some shot glasses. It held no interest for me once I'd outgrown my earlier fascination with opening and closing the escritoire's door to the point of loosening the hinges so much that I was forbidden to come near it again.

The most important segment of the closet was at the bottom. It had three deep shelves that seemed impenetrable to me, and these shelves were filled with books. To see them you had to open two doors, one of which had a key stuck in the lock. The books were arranged in stacks, as many as three or four, starting at the back. Only a few were hardcovers. Most were paperbacks, some of which looked tattered and had loose pages. They must have all been published after the war since neither my mother nor my father had anything that survived. I don't know how many books were there, but if I were to venture a guess I'd say probably a hundred. I don't know, either, if my parents had read all of them. I can assume that they had since they both loved to read. At the time I'm talking about they belonged to the municipal library and went there each week.

I entered that room furtively, even though no one was at home. I tiptoed to the cabinet, squatted, opened one of the bottom doors, and took out the book that I was currently reading. I always left it close to the edge of the shelf, and once I was done with it, I shoved it to the back. That was also the moment when I had to decide what to read next, though this decision was never difficult. I simply pulled out another book as if it were a lottery ticket. Illustrations always spoke in its favor, but ultimately I wanted a book, any book. I laid my prey on one of the chairs surrounding the table—a large oval German affair, with extra leaves underneath—and collected one of the pillows off the couch. I then crawled with the book and the pillow under the table and read until the wooden clock on the wall struck three. That was the signal that if I didn't want to be caught red-handed, it was time to put the book away. The truth was I wouldn't have gotten caught because I locked the door to the apartment from inside and left the key in so that nobody would be able to unlock it from outside. But if I hadn't crawled from under the table early enough, I might have been flustered and blushing, and that might have aroused suspicion.

I can't tell precisely when this clandestine habit began, but certain events allow me to make a decent guess. My grandmother lived with us until I turned ten, and prior to her move she was usually at home when I returned from school. Her presence would have kept me from engaging in my illicit practice. So the proper conditions must have arisen when I entered fifth grade. That was also my younger sister's last year in preschool, which meant that I was alone at home. The following year she started first grade. She would have been done at school each day at 10:35, the time when first graders were let out. I only remember that she was never home when I came back from school about an hour or so later. With her being gone, I could indulge in what quickly became my daily obsession and pleasure.

My parents' book collection was haphazard. A lot of the books were translations from French, which showed my mother's love for French literature. Literary fiction kept company with its more low-brow neighbors. Since back then I would have been unable to make any such aesthetic distinctions, my approach was completely democratic. What I find surprising is how well I remember most of the books I picked up to read. Did my sense of this act's illegitimacy have anything to do with it or was it the tenaciousness of my young mind that accounts for an easy recall of the titles? The first book I ever carried under the table was Benjamin Constant's *Adolphe*. The beat up copy of *The Egyptian* by Mika Waltari came next. I'm not sure about the order of the novels which followed. I recall reading Fennimore Cooper's *The Last of the Mohicans*, a series of historical novels by the Polish writer Józef Ignacy Kraszewski, *The Golden Ass* by Apuleius (which nicely complemented the Greek and Roman myths we read in school), and another historical novel, *The Gadfly*, whose author, Ethel Lilian Voynich, I just now had to look up. Some of the books were appropriate for my age like *The Lost World* by Arthur Conan Doyle, *The Count of Monte Cristo* or even Manon Lescaut and Romain Rolland's *Colas Breugnon.* Some other books like Thomas Hardy's *The Mayor of Casterbridge,* Zola's *Germinal,* or *The Nun* by Denis Diderot were more difficult to follow.

Even though I often didn't understand everything, these works still evoked powerful feelings in me. I plodded through them dutifully and never once quit reading anything I'd started. I would have thought it a betrayal, not so much of the author or the book as of the principles that I was sure all adults adhered to. That may have been the time I decided I was better suited for the life of the mind. I knew books could lead me there, and that they would impart the meaning which at present I craved and only vaguely sensed.

In later years I rarely returned to the books I had read under the table, as if I feared that I'd betray my first love. As a junior in high school, I did reread *Germinal* and *The Nun.* Zola's book was on my reading list, and I reread Diderot's because a friend told me it used to be on the Catholic Church's index of prohibited titles. Since that was the time in my life when I rebelled against prohibitions, I would read anything that was forbidden. I found it exhilarating to delve into a book considered objectionable, particularly by the Church, which I stopped attending after I turned seventeen.

*

When I was growing up, I had no idea that there was censorship in Poland. Few people realized its extent. The authorities took great pains not to call the public's attention to the fact. Much later I found out that right after the war the Ministry of Education sent a confidential letter to public libraries with a list of books that were to be removed from their collections. Such actions were taken in the early 1950s as well to make sure the libraries were purged of all publications that conflicted with the official ideology and party line. The word *cenzura*, however, would have had no meaning for me when I was ten or eleven. My father regularly listened to Radio Free Europe and the Voice of America, and when someone rang the bell or knocked on the door, he'd turn the sound down, say "shush," and only then would he let the visitor in. Depending on who it was, the radio would remain silent or be turned up again. If it was someone trustworthy, a discussion of politics would invariably follow punctuated by the word "they" which referred to party members, the Russians, and some vague and amorphous evil power responsible for all of Poland's woes. My father's other source of news was the newspaper which he read every day only to comment that it was full of lies. I knew lying was bad, and I couldn't figure out why he would be reading something so obviously wicked. Each time I asked him about it, he told me I was too young to understand. As a rule parents avoided involving children in their talks about politics. When a child entered, the adults exchanged meaningful glances and their conversation stalled. I knew there were secrets, and early on I absorbed one lesson: don't ask too many questions and never repeat what was said at home. I heard comments that history books were distorted and teachers had to lie, but I was too savvy to blurt that out at school. Small wonder that my knowledge of Poland's political situation was limited, based on what I managed to overhear. And—to be honest— I wasn't especially interested in it. I had my books, my friends, and knew just enough to keep my mouth shut.

An awakening of sorts happened for me in the last two years of high school, in the aftermath of the March 1968 events. Everyone was talking about student riots in Warsaw, about the cancelled performances of Adam Mickiewicz's play

Forefathers' Eve, about the anti-Semitic hysteria among party apparatchiks that spread to the rank and file and resulted in the exodus from Poland of thousands of Jews. But I became fully aware of the oppressive system we lived under only after I went to college in Wrocław. It's not that I joined an opposition group and got enlightened there. My classmates and I talked a lot about politics and shared numerous political jokes. Politics, however, wasn't the focus of our lives. At least not at first.

Since we majored in English, through the grapevine we heard the story of our department, which was affected by some seismic shocks in Poland's post-WWII history. When the university re-opened its doors in 1945, the English department had its place within the School of Humanities, and nobody would think to dispute its existence. Five years later the communist authorities decided to close down suspect departments such as English, French, Oriental languages, as well as Slavics, which got replaced with Russian. After the 1956 thaw, the French department reopened, while English— which, according to the Party ideologues, represented hostile imperialist countries—remained closed until 1965. Over the next five years a few professors were hired, and in 1970, the reconstituted department admitted its first students. I began attending the university a year later.

The departmental library was still at the old 1940s location. I remember very well the day on which we were asked to help move the whole collection of books to the new space that the department now occupied. After we finished, sweaty and covered with dust, we were rewarded with some of the books that had been sentenced to the trash pile, possibly for the sole reason that they bore the prewar German stamps of the university library, since Wrocław was the old German city of Breslau, a fact that the communists tried to eradicate from people's memory. Hence, as invariably happened, politics won over common sense. I ended up with a couple of beautiful nineteenth-century editions of *Henry IV* and *Richard II*. The added irony was that our departmental library had very few books at the time because the university authorities allotted little money for English-language texts. We couldn't check them out—there were too few copies for everyone—and students had to put their names on a list, waiting their turn to read. Only late on Friday night, right when the library was closing, were we permitted to carry the coveted book home.

When I traveled to England for the first time in 1973, I worked illegally as a waitress and spent most of the money I earned on books that we'd already read for class but which I had fallen in love with and wanted to own. They were mainly British nineteenth-century classics like *Pride and Prejudice*, *Wuthering Heights*, and *Jane Eyre*. As a responsible student, I also bought the books for the next year. I envied the British people that they could walk into a bookstore and get anything they wanted, that no one would try to interfere with how and what they read. By that time I was familiar with censorship and knew the names of the writers who for political reasons weren't published in Poland and whose works were prohibited. Carrying such books into the country, I'd risk their confiscation at the border, but I was willing to take that risk. I purchased *Cancer Ward* by Solzhenitsyn, Orwell's *Homage to Catalonia*, and Huxley's *Brave New World*. While the ban on Solzhenitsyn could easily be explained—the book was an unveiled allegory of totalitarianism and offered a scathing criticism of Soviet society, something even a dumb censor would pick up—the ban on Orwell and Huxley was more troubling, because it drew attention to a facet of censorship I would have rather ignored: the interpretive intelligence of its lackeys. And then there was Czesław Miłosz. An old Polish man, a WWII veteran, had once invited me to his house for dinner and given me Miłosz's *Widzenia nad Zatoką San Francisco* (*Visions from San Francisco Bay*), which was published in Paris by the Polish émigré journal *Kultura*. Miłosz was persona non grata in Poland, and his books were only available abroad.

Before returning home from England, I packed carefully, trying to devise ways to outsmart the border control. I had the culprits mixed in with the innocents, and placed the Miłosz book in my oversized purse. The border agents took away the Solzhenitsyn novel, and ignored everything else, laughing out loud that instead of bringing useful items that were in permanent short supply, someone could be so foolish as to haul a suitcase of books. I faked outraged innocence, and that's how my first face-to-face encounter with censorship ended.

A year or so later I was renting a room from a woman whose Warsaw cousin came for a visit. While she was at work, he was busily typing something on her old typewriter, and one day proudly handed me a smudged carbon copy of Leszek Kołakowski's essay "Tezy o nadziei i beznadziejności" ("Theses on Hope and Hopelessness"). He didn't say a word. He only placed his index finger on his lips to indicate the need for secrecy. That was my first exposure to *samizdat*. In the late 1970s those publications became easily available, and thanks to them I read Miłosz's *The Captive Mind* and his poems, which appeared officially in print only after he won the Nobel Prize in 1980. By then the authorities who'd sentenced him to oblivion could no longer pretend Miłosz didn't exist. During the short period of Solidarity ascension, clandestine publications flourished, as if for a change the authorities had decided to give people more carrot than stick. Afterwards, under Martial Law, the Party was again wielding its stick, or perhaps I should say a whip, which had replaced the somewhat gentler tools of repression. Nothing could be printed or copied, and even typewriters were confiscated for fear they might be used for anti-military pamphlets. This was a grim time that to this day I can only recall with a shudder.

*

In 1992, by which time I had already been living in the United States for eight years and had two daughters, ages three and four, my husband Steve got a sabbatical from the university he taught at, and the whole family spent the fall semester in Poland. Since our daughters were bilingual, I read Polish children's books to them and he read to them in English. While we were in Poland, I taught our older daughter, Antonina, to read in Polish. On returning home to America, she had her first opportunity to realize what power the ability to read conferred. Both girls wanted to go to McDonald's and have the children's meal which came with a toy. Steve didn't feel like driving all the way to the nearest Golden Arches, so he took them instead to a much closer Carl's Junior, convinced they wouldn't know the difference. On arrival Antonina turned to him and said, "This isn't McDonald's. It's Carl's Junior." She pronounced the name as "Tsarls Yunior," the way a Polish child would.

She quickly learned to read in English too, and in no time was devouring books the way I did when I was her age. The younger one, Magdalena, struggled at first and often asked me to read to her. I obliged, read a page or two, and then claimed my eyes felt tired. If she wanted to know what would happen, she'd have to take over. She read falteringly, but daily practice helped, and when she was in third grade she took off on her own. Both girls became avid readers who would read "kiddy stuff," as they called it, side by side with adult fare. Like my parents, we let them choose whatever they wanted. Unlike my parents, however, we spent a lot of time talking with them about books. Occasionally, when each family member brought a book to the lunch or dinner table and was forlornly cradling it in his or her lap, we would break the sacrosanct rule against reading at meals.

For a long time after I arrived in America I couldn't get over the ease of acquiring books. I bought or ordered them through a local bookstore, and each time I did, I recalled the trouble I had to go to in Poland when I wanted a particular title. The best strategy was to befriend someone who worked at a bookstore. Once that happened, you could count on them to keep new arrivals under the counter for you and their other friends. After the friends made their selection, the leftover books would be displayed for other customers. Everyone was familiar with the term "from under the counter," which referred to any choice products, not only books.

Our daughters never had to resort to getting books "from under the counter" or felt the urge to read under the table. Even though some American parents went to great lengths to censor books at schools and libraries, and keep their children from reading my daughters' beloved *Pippi*, the *Harry Potter* series, or the hilarious and scary Roald Dahl, my children were raised in an open society where information passes unobstructed, where adults aren't wary of what children can overhear, and people typically place a finger across their lips to indicate that someone may be taking a nap. They had no need for secrecy except for secrets that one friend passed to another.

*

When I think of my own childhood, I wonder why I ever created my elaborate clandestine ritual. My parents wouldn't have considered censoring my reading and always allowed me complete autonomy. Most of the time they had no idea what I read. Only infrequently, when they questioned the fulfillment of their parental obligations, or—more likely—when they couldn't get my attention, would one of them ask what book I was buried in. If I had requested one of the books that had been kept in the bottom cabinet and was officially theirs, they would have happily handed me whichever one I desired. On some level I must have known that all along, yet I practiced stealth and secrecy. Maybe I wanted to have my own secret that would let me feel special and privileged, different from other children who spent hours outside playing noisily and happily. By then I had already figured out that reading was a vital component of my happiness.

Choosing concealment may also have been my way of showing defiance. While I accomplished rebellious feats in my imagination, in real life I was an obedient child who tended to follow rules and was well-behaved. I convinced myself that what I was doing was devious and out of bounds, and I was proud that I showed my mettle by engaging in such risky behavior whose added bonus was the excitement it infused into my proper and predictable daily life. For me, the act itself, not the content of the books I read, had the aura of the forbidden. I wasn't skimming them in search of racy details and scenes. To begin with I was too innocent to know what to look for.

Since I often read difficult books, without fully comprehending the text, I entered the world of a particular novel and exited it without the full knowledge of that world, the kind of knowledge that an older reader would have acquired. In some way this experience mirrored my life at the time. Just like its fictional reflection, the real world was mysterious, amazing, and promising. Once I grew up, it would spread all its riches before me as though on the magic tablecloth that appeared in many of my favorite fairy tales. If I was aware of my perceptual and intellectual gaps, I didn't think it was a problem. But now I can say that the foundation for my future reading life was being laid then. Maybe I began to discover that certain books surrender grudgingly and permit the reader only brief flashes of meaning and that—as is the case in the world at large—some

things should better be left alone, glimpsed but not examined
or explained away.

I've tried many times to determine when I gave up my
secret undertaking, but memory refuses to yield reliable
specifics. My habit may have petered out on its own when
social life at school became important to me. Or I may have
at last admitted to myself the absurdity of it when my mother
opened the cabinet, took out *The Doll*, a novel by Bolesław
Prus, and told me I would love it. There may have also been
another, more mundane reason, which could have taken
precedence over the other two. I remember that at one point
my parents decided to get rid of the ponderous post-German
furniture and replace it with more modern, lighter stuff. They
sold the cabinet, and the huge table that had sheltered me,
unaware that with one stroke they deprived me of my happiest
hours, of my dose of imaginative nourishment, my daily secret
devouring.

EUROPA, EUROPA

In 1990, a year after the first democratic elections in Poland, I was visiting Wrocław, the city where I used to live. I went to lunch at a newly opened vegetarian restaurant with an old friend, and she brought along another friend, the woman who gave me Italian lessons when we were both college students. She had left Poland two years after graduating and had lived in Zurich ever since. We talked about the changes that were taking place in our native country, and at one point the Swiss émigré remarked that she now viewed herself as a European rather than a Pole. If she had asserted her allegiance to Switzerland, I wouldn't have been puzzled. I knew immigrants who almost immediately claimed their new country as their own, as if making that decision would free them from homesickness and nostalgia and help them more quickly fashion a new start in life. But she was claiming the whole continent. Was she trying to put on cosmopolitan airs and show her superiority to those who, like my Wrocław friend, were watching the difficult birth of Poland's democracy?

At the time of that encounter, I had lived in the United States for six years, and it may have been too soon for me to contemplate the shifts in identity engendered by immigration. But several years later, I too began to use the term *European* to describe myself, a change set in motion, paradoxically, by my interactions with fellow Americans who classified me as a European long before I did. When I said something that seemed odd or expressed an opinion that went counter to theirs, they ascribed it to my European upbringing instead of my predilections or idiosyncrasies as they would have done with their American-born friends. A banal remark that I disliked gyms or didn't want chips served with my sandwich would often produce a comment whose gist was that my views and tastes only confirmed my European origins. In those casual exchanges I never attempted to tell them I had friends in Europe who religiously attended gyms or that many people there happily munched chips. It didn't bother me that I was thrown into a common European sack. A European, to them, represented a distillation of the national characteristics they associated with France, Germany, Italy, Spain—the more familiar countries of Western Europe. On many occasions when I said I was from Poland, people would nod, smile, and assign me to Holland, a country whose name they readily recognized.

Over time, my own outlook changed. Living in America granted me the privilege of the outsider, which allowed for a broader vision. As I gradually exited my own language and culture, I began to feel I could no longer be contained solely within the categories of Polishness. I first noticed that when I ceased comparing American reality to the one I had left behind in Poland and began to use Europe as my frame of reference. It's as though I had to live here to feel European. Despite my numerous emotional and personal ties to this country, I knew early on that I would never feel American. I'm not trying to be contrary when I say so. I can relate to the experience of my immigrant friends who tell me they feel American heart and soul. That just hasn't been my experience. I appreciate America the way Gertrude Stein appreciated France when she famously said, "It is not what France gave you but what it did not take from you that was important." I was allowed to remain who I am and never felt any pressure to transform myself into someone I was not.

*

If I had used the label *European* when I still lived in Poland, it would have been ironic. Geography assigned me and my countrymen to Europe, but we didn't quite feel part of this larger whole. We were shaped by being, as it were, at the crossroads. Eastern Europe might have been European in its mentality and culture, as Milan Kundera so often pointed out in his essays, but we were the continent's farthest outpost, shackled to the East. De Gaulle's optimistic assessment that Europe stretched all the way to the Urals sounded to us like a bad joke. While Europe meant human rights and democracy, we viewed such ideals as a distant and impossible dream. The shabbiness of our everyday lives was a constant and painful reminder of our true position. The West to us was better and more European than the Europe in which we lived under Soviet domination, under a political system which called itself communist democracy, an oxymoron typical of the Party's predilection for Newspeak.

Not that we didn't want to belong to Europe. To sustain the belief in our European identity, flawed as it was, we kept reminding ourselves of the heritage we shared with the West. But even the attempts of Kundera to differentiate us from our oppressors by using the term *Central* to describe us did little to dispel our doubts and make us feel like equal members of the European family. We never felt central. We were relegated to the periphery.

Whenever our more fortunate cousins from Western countries came to visit, they viewed us at best as poor relatives. In a letter to Hannah Arendt, Mary McCarthy, who visited Poland in November, 1960, wrote that she saw "mass Poland in a pure state: the colorless crowds milling along the grey streets, the shops and restaurants all alike and all carrying the same products, the bookstores with the same books." We didn't need our foreign guests to tell us how they saw us. We knew that to them we looked like uncouth barbarians, and that the surface grayness turned us into the dull other who merited little or no attention.

If we were lucky to travel to the West—and I use the word *lucky* to express the unpredictability of the endeavor—our clothes, suitcases, and other paraphernalia made most of us immediately recognizable as hailing from the "other" Europe. The moment we had some spending money from grants, stipends, or illegal labor, we immediately purchased new attire, ridding ourselves of Soviet bloc-style jeans, T-shirts, jackets, or shoes. But this dream metamorphosis into a Westerner didn't work. Our brand-new clothes drew attention to their newness. In our unblemished sneakers, fresh T-shirts, and stiff jeans, we stood out around the casually dressed natives. An English friend once told me he could always spot Eastern Europeans even after they'd stayed in London for a while.

Those of us who had interest in higher culture could also be easily identified in bookstores and museums. We'd spend hours browsing the shelves, picking up books, opening them, reading a few pages here and there, calculating how many we could afford. I remember going to a bookstore in Cambridge on three consecutive days before I made my final decision and hauled away a full backpack; this was such a heady experience that at the checkout I forgot my wallet with hard-earned money from waitressing and had to return the next day. In a museum we were the ones who came in right when it opened and left a few minutes before it closed. Our hunger was so great that we skipped lunch to give ourselves more time. We wanted to see it all since we might never be able to return.

A friend who studied Romance languages at the University of Warsaw told me about her first trip to Paris. She divided the city into sections that she planned to see, making sure she wouldn't miss anything. She decided to devote three days to the Louvre. She went there early in the morning, and by the evening of the first day she was dazzled and dizzy, her head spinning. She figured right then that it made no sense to try to see everything, but a voice kept whispering, "What if next year you don't get a passport?" Another voice, the voice of Eastern European fatalism, went even further: "What if this won't be here anymore?" She repeated to herself the lines from Zbigniew Herbert's poem "Mona Lisa," like an incantation—"so I'm here you see I'm here I hadn't a hope but I'm here." Unreformed, she stuck to her plans. On the third day she spent a lot of time in front of Caravaggio's *Death of the Virgin*, and then returned to the room two more times. Finally, she became aware that the security guard was eyeing her suspiciously as if she were plotting to steal the painting.

We always wanted to know what was happening on the other side of the Iron Curtain, what books got published, what movies were made, what exhibitions had just opened in London, Barcelona, or Munich. If our complexes played some role in our desire to keep abreast of the cultural developments abroad, they weren't the main reason. Seeing a new Buñuel movie which had at last made its way into Poland, attending a Peter Brook performance, or reading the latest Julio Cortázar novel gave us a semblance of freedom—we could pretend, even if only for a short time, that we were part of the "normal" world. More important, though, it created a sphere of genuine spiritual freedom, a sphere no one could encroach on. In 1963, when the first Polish translation of Joyce's *Ulysses* was published, winding lines formed in front of bookstores. One might think this was nothing but snobbery, and it's possible that some buyers were driven by the book's snob appeal; there's no data on how many of the people who had bought the book actually read it. But anyone who discounts our hunger doesn't understand its nature, as the sated never understand the starving.

Thanks to such cravings, aesthetic or not, we knew a lot about other European countries and the rest of the world, not just about the major players like France and Germany and the United States. That knowledge now and then gave us a fleeting feeling of superiority as we marveled at the ignorance of those who lived in better places. But most of the time we loved them and admired them even when there was little to admire, as if we equated democracy with goodness and morality. Sadly, it was an unreciprocated love, since few of them knew much about us or cared to know. Only riots or rebellions reminded them of our existence. Otherwise, people from Eastern Europe were indistinguishable fish swimming in a muddy totalitarian pool.

In August 1980, when shipyard strikes began in Gdańsk and the Solidarity movement was born, I was living in West Berlin and working at an ice cream shop. My time there was coming to an end and I wanted to spend a week in England before returning home. To save money, I hitchhiked to the Netherlands to catch a ferry. My first ride took me to Braunschweig, and then a Dutchman traveling with his small daughter drove me all the way to Hooek van Holland, where the ferry docked. We talked about what was happening in Poland, and whether the Soviets might intervene. I was worried yet hopeful. The driver was concerned about the possible impact on the rest of Europe, which to him was Western Europe. He thought the workers should stop their strikes and go back to work to placate Poland's neighbor to the East. I knew there were numerous Western Europeans as exhilarated and hopeful as we in Poland were. But that encounter made me realize that there were also those to whom we posed a threat. As long as their own safety and well-being weren't at stake, they were all for freedom and democracy, and believed that all people were equal. And yet even an imaginary and distant danger led them to draw a distinction between more and less equal Europeans.

*

If I were asked what Europe means to me, the first and most obvious thing I could say would be its cultural and intellectual heritage, which molded my beliefs, sensibilities, morals, and aesthetic sense. Everywhere in Europe I find reminders of my country's history and the history it shared with the rest of the continent. Its architecture, art, music, and literature, those highly quotable manifestations of European essence, evoke many sentimental associations for me. Then there are the everyday things—shops, trains, streetcars, people on foot in every city, open-air markets—which make a person from Lisbon feel at home in Prague or a Dubliner comfortable among the crowds on a street in Tallinn. These are the charms and lures of the old continent recognized by natives and outsiders, Europe at its best.

But there's an underside to this perfect image. There's one Europe, but its eastern part is still Eastern with only Western icing on top. After years of totalitarianism, democracy doesn't happen overnight, even if overnight people are free to vote in democratic elections. It is a long process that involves changes in attitudes. The standard of living in the West is still—and for many years will be—much higher than in the East. We in the East may now buy Chanel N°5, only to discover it was made in China. What is considered normal in the West is often a luxury in the East, and I mean such trivial things as well-running and clean trains, people picking up after their dogs, the absence of drunks on park benches. No matter what EU officials claim, the national interests of each European country take precedence over the interests of Europe as a whole. Tolerance goes only so far if a newcomer from what used to be the Other Europe competes with the natives for a job or if the wealthier countries have to open their wallets to salvage the poorer ones. Nationalistic phobias are still stoked by populist politicians. The Iron Curtain is gone, but it will take years, if not generations, before other barriers disappear. European officials love to talk about a Europe of homelands, but it's difficult to forget the two world wars, tens of millions dead, the Holocaust, the Bosnian massacre, all accomplished in the name of homelands.

The year Poland joined the European Union was also celebrated as the Year of Witold Gombrowicz. The Polish parliament issued a special decree to honor the one hundredth anniversary of the great writer's birth. The coincidence contained a poignant irony, not lost on his Polish readers. Gombrowicz, whose writings show a lifelong obsession with Polishness, urged his fellow countrymen to face Europe without provincial complexes, years before anyone could even dream of the changes that were coming. Despite his emotional ties to Poland, he saw himself as a cosmopolitan and a European and mocked his native country's collective subjugation to national pieties and mythologies. In 2004 we thought of the value of the lesson of Gombrowicz for the Polish people. Today Gombrowicz should be required reading in other European countries, particularly when the beast of nationalism raises its head again.

By this reckoning and in view of Europe's most recent troubles, I should have little hope for Europe, but that's not the case. Someone may call me naïve, but I believe in the idea of Europe. Paul Valéry expressed my sentiments and probably the sentiments of others when in one of his essays he said that a European combines a pessimistic view of human experience, of people, and of life, with action and optimism, because action requires optimism. The demons of the past haven't all been exorcised, though in recent years I've noticed some positive signs. More and more people from my part of the world, particularly the younger ones, call themselves European, without a trace of self-consciousness or irony. If the test of their allegiance to the idea of Europe would be to die for it, they would fail it—but then they'd rather not die for their own countries either. My conception of Europe is burdened by the fact that I was born before the Iron Curtain was dismantled. The new generation of Central Europeans is free of such baggage. If their better-off cousins had committed grave sins against their parents and grandparents, those wrongs have been forgotten. Young people on both sides of the former divide now learn each other's languages, watch foreign TV stations, work for multi-national companies, travel and study abroad. And the European Union, this behemoth obsessed with common measurements for agricultural machinery or uniform standards for dairy products, does a lot through its educational programs to promote cultural exchange and understanding. European youth are now more familiar with other countries than previous generations. The exchange described in Wisława Szymborska's poem "Vocabulary"—"La Pologne? La Pologne? Isn't it terribly cold there?"—is unlikely to take place among them.

Our daughter lived for three years in Poland teaching English at one of Kraków's private language schools. The city is full of young people from all over Europe who live and work there, play music in bars and cafés, publish English-language newspapers. She had friends from Germany, the Netherlands, Italy, Scotland, Ireland. For a while, her best friend was a young woman from Finland, who spent two years in Poland, taught herself the language, and then went on to study at the University of Glasgow. The parents of one of our daughter's roommates, a native Pole, had moved to Spain when he was four. Their son is perfectly bilingual, speaks flawless English, and was studying toward a PhD in translation at the Jagiellonian University. Her South African boyfriend, who also has British citizenship and who later became her husband, participated in the European Union's Erasmus Mundus program, studied for one year at University College, London, then went to Kraków to finish his MA at the local university. These young people know their history but seem unencumbered by it. They don't view Europe in terms of borders, resentments, or grudges. They focus on and revel in what they have in common.

*

Stanisław Vincenz, a writer who was born in southeastern Poland, dreamed of a Europe of provinces. For him a homeland wasn't a country but a smaller region where people felt connected to each other and to the place. Europe has always had its different local patriotisms, but today there's an even greater interest in the local scale, in what Czesław Miłosz called "the small homelands." This phenomenon is easily observed even in the former People's Republics where under Soviet rule centralization was an act of faith. After the initial intoxication with everything foreign, I now see in Poland an increasing pride in what's native—from cheeses, vodka, beer, music, to local history and traditions. By supporting these new trends with subsidies, the EU contributes more and more to the high value placed on regions and their communities.

I doubt that nations will ever disappear. I think the concept will grow less important within Europe and the role of large homelands will be taken over by small ones. The "nation" is increasingly difficult to define. Unified Europe is supposed to connect different nations, yet we all know that history in its national dimension tends to divide. But the autonomy and separateness of small homelands provoke few divisive emotions. Maybe that's what the future Europe will be like—a Europe of provinces, where people will be proud of their communities, their small homelands, and will also identify with Europe, the bigger entity of which they will remain a part.

If you set out on a journey let it be long
wandering that seems to have no aim groping your way blindly
so you learn the roughness of the earth not only with your eyes
but by touch
so you confront the world with your whole skin
                                        —Zbigniew Herbert, "Journey"

IN ZBIGNIEW HERBERT'S GARDEN

For many years I believed that the great Polish poet Zbigniew
Herbert traveled by bus to the places he describes in *Barbarian
in the Garden*. Each time I re-read *Barbarian* I could picture
him wearing a white shirt, sleeves rolled up, wiping sweat off
his forehead, and climbing onto a dust-covered bus. Since
I had no clue what an Italian bus would have looked like at
the time of Herbert's journeys, it invariably resembled the
dilapidated Polish buses I used to ride as a child in the late
Fifties and early Sixties, and the background I envisioned

could have come straight from a Rosellini or a De Sica movie. The problem is that in the entire book he makes only a few references to his manner of travel: we know, for example, that he went to Lascaux and Chaalis by bus, and to Paestum and Orvieto by train. Most of the essays begin after he's already arrived at a given destination, allowing the reader to get the gist of things much sooner than if the author had cluttered his essays with minute details of his arrivals and departures. I'm sure that I could have settled the question once and for all if I'd had a scholar's yen for research. But the lack of textual evidence that would corroborate my theory didn't bother me at all. The bus just had to be Herbert's preferred means of transportation. How else could he have gone from one little Tuscan or Umbrian town to another?

To begin with, I reasoned, buses are cheaper than trains, and it is a well-known fact that when Herbert first went abroad, he traveled on a shoestring. Back then even people who had a lot of money in Poland—and Herbert didn't—couldn't use it for travel to the West, because Polish currency was worthless outside our country's borders. None of the Eastern Bloc currencies were exchangeable into Western money. One could buy dollars on the black market, but the procedure was illegal, and taking foreign money out of the country was tantamount to smuggling. Polish citizens were allowed to carry only ten dollars with them, a measly sum that wouldn't be enough for one day in Western Europe. They also had to list the amount of money they took out and brought back into Poland on the so-called currency declaration. After one of his trips, when Herbert was interrogated by the secret police, he was asked how it was possible that he'd left Poland with five dollars, spent six months abroad, and still managed to return with three dollars. Without batting an eye he said, "I saved." The man in the dark suit knew that the poet had been relying on awards and grants from Western cultural institutions and hoped he would admit that. But such an admission would have meant opening Pandora's box. Polish Communist authorities loved to accuse people of collaborating with foreign agencies, an accusation that in its mildest form would result in the denial of a passport.

So even though those awards and grants allowed Herbert to live in the West for long periods of time, he had to budget his money carefully. In *Barbarian in the Garden* he often comments on his meager funds. At lunchtime in Siena he says, "I make a quick calculation and learn that I can afford only a cup of coffee and a piece of bread with ham." In Paris, wishing to see the cathedral at Chartres, he goes on Sunday to benefit from "reduced fares." Seeing Chartres makes him abandon his original plan to write a dissertation on Paul Valéry. Instead, he decides to visit all the French cathedrals, "an insane plan," as he admits. Wherever he goes, he has little money but a huge appetite. He has to stretch his franc, pound, or lira if he wants to see it all. And he wants to see it all. This kind of hunger may be incomprehensible to a person raised in the comforts of Western democracies. After all, if on one trip you miss Piero della Francesca's *The Legend of the True Cross* in Arezzo, it will be there next time you go. For a person from the old Eastern Bloc, however, the next time might not have been there. Before Communism's downfall, we never kept our passports shoved into the drawer between last year's tax returns and a college diploma, ready to be used whenever we contracted a traveling bug. We had to depend on the good graces of dour secret police (masquerading as passport bureau officials) to issue us the necessary travel documents, and once we got them, we could never be sure we'd get them again. So if we were allowed to leave the best of all possible worlds where we were condemned to live, we wanted to make the most of each trip to the West.

Another argument that I had mustered in favor of buses was that they can go where trains can't or don't. Trains might do for a conventional tourist who follows the predictable itinerary suggested by his guidebook. But Herbert was anything but conventional, even in his choice of guidebooks. When he traveled in Italy and France, he carried a 1909 *Guide to Europe* published by the Academic Touring Club in Lvov, which had come from his father's library. For his travels in the Netherlands he used a Baedeker from 1911. He didn't care for novelty. He believed that "one should not surrender to the dictatorship of guidebooks." One shouldn't begin one's visit from three-starred places but "from a godforsaken province abandoned and orphaned by history." He had prepared meticulously for each trip and would often visit places that only the initiated would know about, like Monterchi, a village some miles away from Arezzo, whose chapel housed a fresco by Piero della Francesca. But knowing what he wanted to see never kept him from welcoming "chance and adventure."

And finally, I told myself, buses were much more democratic, no first-class coach there, no fancy restaurant cars. Herbert, "an irresistible charmer," as some friends called him, was a people person, at ease with a shepherd in Sparta or a trattoria owner in Perugia. In a letter he sent to Czeslaw Milosz in July 1969, he jokingly remarks that his love of classicism was responsible for his drinking with some sailors from Pireus in a bar in Ravenna until it closed. So Herbert just had to prefer the down-to-earth atmosphere and the congeniality of a bus.

*

I first read *Barbarian in the Garden* when I was a second-year art history student at the University of Wrocław in Poland. That spring semester I had a class in the Italian Renaissance. The professor assigned us a substantial reading list for the course, most of it comprising standard books and articles. I was surprised when I spotted Herbert's book on the list—I knew him as a poet but not as an essayist. Immediately after class I went to a second-hand bookstore in Wrocław's market square and was lucky to find there a 1973 edition of *Barbarian*, which had first come out in Poland in 1962. I've had the same old book ever since, and I brought it with me when I came to America.

I began reading the book while riding a streetcar back home, and continued late into the night. Herbert held me spellbound. After dry academic textbooks with little passion or flair, *Barbarian in the Garden* was a dazzling revelation. A traveler's account, imaginative and erudite, it looked at art and life and took the reader to art's salons and kitchens. Then and there I decided I'd one day travel to all these places Herbert described and see things through his eyes. The place I most wanted to visit was Italy, but history played havoc with my plans. It was twenty years before I ever set foot in Florence. By then I knew that my imaginary trip would never materialize and that my earlier theory on Herbert and buses was just a theory. By then, too, the political circumstances in my part of Europe were radically different from the times when he first traveled abroad.

*

When Herbert left Poland in the late 1950s during the post-Stalinist thaw, he left a country in the throes of totalitarian ugliness, full of the deafening din of official lies and ideology. People from the Soviet Bloc dreamed of going to the West, but that dream came true for only a few. Some of those who were fortunate enough to obtain a passport never returned, or "chose freedom," as we euphemistically and sometimes enviously used to call it. Like so many of us, they simply longed for a sense of normality and for day-to-day lives that weren't choked by politics.

Herbert could easily have stayed in the West, joining the ranks of numerous other dissident writers who defected. Each time the Communist authorities granted him a passport they must have hoped he would never come back. However, he always returned "to the stony bosom of his homeland." He wanted to escape "the places of...[his] daily torment," but his escapes, longer and shorter, were only temporary. Everyday life in Poland was unpredictable, formless, shoddy, and glum. It wouldn't be an exaggeration to say that his desire to escape was motivated by his yearning for beauty, harmony, permanence, and solidity, qualities sorely missing from a part of the world where everything became oddly intertwined with politics.

The Old Masters provided an escape. Yet Herbert's journeys into the world of painting and architecture were never a retreat from the quotidian world. Herbert prided himself on his no-nonsense attitude and his devotion to the concrete. Discussing the Gothic cathedrals, he promises the reader "a simple goal, an accountant's view." Arriving in Holland, he declares: "The romantic Mr. Fromentin spins out meditations about lofty things, history, beauty, fame. I, however, cling to the brick." For him art and life are part of the same fabric of human experience. He believes that "the ideal traveler knows how to enter into contact with nature, with people and their history as well as their art. Only familiarity with these three overlapping elements can be the starting point of knowledge about a country." This lover of antiquity, this classicist, wants to immerse himself in the everyday life of the places he visits as much as he longs to see the masterpieces that have remained the same for centuries.

Herbert does not just cursorily look at works of art like most tourists do: he studies them, tries to commit them to memory, sketches them. His drawings show that he was an accomplished artist. He studied at the Academy of Fine Arts in Kraków until a professor told him there wasn't much more he could learn but a lot that could ruin his individual style. And on his trips he put his talent to good use, always walking around with a sketchbook and drawing what he saw. He knew that each visit might be the last one. "This is my last evening in Siena. I go to the Campo to throw a few lire into the Fonte Gaia, though to tell the truth, I have little hope of returning," he says in his essay on Siena in *Barbarian*. He appreciates his good luck, and his joy at being able to see what others less fortunate have been denied finds its way into his poems, essays, and letters. In June 1959 he sent Czesław Miłosz a postcard on which he says, "So I am in Italy, that is to say, down on my knees, at the source. I live in Spoleto, a small Umbrian town." A year later he reports to Miłosz, "I'm writing now a book of reports from Italy and France." That book of "reports" was *Barbarian in the Garden*.

*

Wherever Herbert traveled in Europe, he felt at home. Yet this consummate European also called himself a barbarian. Was it because he felt that he was somehow different? It couldn't have been anything as trivial or external as a foreign accent, clothes, or behavior, even though people from behind the Iron Curtain showed all the telltale signs of living on its wrong side. In *Travels with Herodotus* Ryszard Kapuściński writes that on his way to India via Rome, he was aware that he looked like someone who was out of place, dressed as he was in the style à la Warsaw Pact. After he bought himself a new suit, shirt, and tie, he continued to feel the stares of others when he sat at a café. Now he looked like an oddity because of his all-too-noticeable brand-new clothes. But Herbert never paid much attention to attire and most likely wouldn't have noticed it if someone gave him a funny look. His sartorial taste was limited to practical items. He spent his money on museums, food, and hotels. He never stayed at expensive places, since one night there could have paid for three or four nights at a less fancy establishment. In Naples he stays at the Albergo Fiore "for both patriotic reasons (the owner was a compatriot) and ulterior motives (it was cheap)." In Siena he chooses the modest Tre Donzelle that, even after being renovated, has remained modest to this day.

It's tempting to assume that he calls himself a barbarian because he hails from "the other"—Eastern—Europe, but that explanation isn't true for Herbert. No matter where he travels—from the Acropolis, to Chartres, to Hadrian's Wall— he claims European culture as his own, and all his travels only confirm his sense of belonging to it. Returning from Lascaux, he muses: "Though I had stared into the 'abyss' of history, I did not emerge from an alien world. Never before had I felt a stronger or more reassuring conviction: I am a citizen of the earth, an inheritor not only of the Greeks and Romans but of almost the whole infinity."

So his choice of the word "barbarian" couldn't have been motivated by the complexes or coyness of a poor relative from the provinces. To Herbert we're simply all barbarians when we enter art's garden. We're also barbarians in the Greek sense of the word because each traveler is always "the other," an intruder of sorts who observes the newly encountered world with a certain detachment. Anyone who has ever traveled knows that we don't experience the reality of the places we travel to the way their residents experience it. On foreign soil we're no longer mastered by our indignation at corrupt politicians, moronic bureaucrats, the absurd rules and regulations that dog our daily lives. The locals may—and, in fact, usually do—have their own share of problems, but we're not responsible for them. We have left all that behind; our rage and guilt too are on vacation. Now and then, though, we may feel estranged, and Herbert is well aware of that. He comments on this feeling in *Still Life with a Bridle* (which has been translated into English by John and Bogdana Carpenter): "An attack of alienation, but a gentle one that touches most people transported into a foreign place." But he views this otherness as something positive that allows the traveler to notice what natives can no longer see. Freed from habit and routine, the traveler is in a heightened state of mindfulness because "in a state of alienation the eyes react quickly to objects and banal events that do not exist for the practical eye." Traveling thus becomes a honeymoon for the senses, when predictable responses are replaced by fresh perceptions and a feeling of awe, even at the sight of "small street fragments of reality."

When we travel, otherness has two senses: we're obviously "the other," but the world we encounter is also "the other." And even though it may be bewildering, Herbert believes we should reach out to that otherness. In his short essay "Mr. Montaigne's Travel to Italy," which hasn't been translated into English, he acknowledges that it's more difficult for the modern traveler "to mix in with the concrete otherness of the landscape, the people, and the events" than it was in Montaigne's lifetime. Today's traveler is protected from the quotidian life by "the international hotel, the conventionality of tourism, guidebooks, a hurried contact with notable objects, the injunction to commune with universal works and not with the incomparable, distinctive beauty of life."

Herbert had none of the protections he mentions—but then he never desired them. He wanted to be protected *from* them. "If the gods protect one from organized tours (through insufficient funds or strong character)," he says in *Barbarian*, "one should spend the first hours in a new city following a simple rule: straight ahead, third left, straight ahead, third right." The gods always looked out for him, sparing him the indignities of being a conventional tourist and allowing him to follow his own fancy. He travels leisurely, with plenty of unplanned stops and detours, watching life unfold and trying to blend in with the surrounding otherness. Even though he often tells himself he must be on his way, he has time to observe a lizard, to notice "the color of mailboxes, tramways, knockers on doors," to listen to a street organ. Anywhere he goes, he indulges in "the most pleasant item on the schedule—loafing around," just as he does after his visit to the cathedral at Senlis:

> wandering aimlessly...staring...picking up pebbles and throwing them away, drinking wine in the darkest spots: Chez Jean, Petit Vatel...smiling at girls, putting your face to walls to catch their smells...joining a dice game, visiting an antique shop and asking the price of an ebony music box...studying the menus in the windows of exclusive restaurants and indulging in licentious fantasies: lobster or oysters for starters; careful reading of the fete's programme and the list of prizes to be won in tombola for the soldiers, and all the other notices, especially those written by hand.

Just as he doesn't believe in "the rapid swallowing of paintings," he takes his time enjoying local food. His descriptions of art in *Barbarian* are followed by descriptions of the delights of the palate. This Olympian of high taste was obviously someone to whom the pleasures of eating were not foreign. Living under Communism rarely led to a refined taste in food, unless, like Herbert, one was a sensualist and a natural gourmet. On his way to Lascaux, he stops at the small village of Montignac for breakfast and raves about an omelette—"an omelette with truffles is delicious and their smell, as the dish has no taste, is incomparable." Then he follows with a brief lecture on truffles. After viewing the paintings of Simone Martini and Ambrogio Lorenzetti in Siena, Herbert offers gushing praise of pizza, which he learned to love in Naples, and later describes the sensation of drinking Campari. Before leaving Siena he regales the reader with a detailed explanation of how one should drink wine—instruction that no winery owner whose family has been in the business of wine-making for centuries could surpass. When in Arles, he extols the glories of Provençal cooking: "First comes a tin tray with hors d'oeuvres: green and black olives, pickles, endives, and spicy potatoes. Then the delicious fish soup, a cousin of the queen of soups—the bouillabaisse of Marseilles."

When Herbert comes to Orvieto, his writing about food reaches its heights. Never sentimental when he writes about art, he sounds ecstatic describing the local wine:

> On the menu I find a wine named after the town. The *padrone* praises it more loudly than the cathedral... It is more difficult to describe the wine than the cathedral. It is the color of straw and has a strong, elusive aroma. The first sip is rather unimpressive. The effect starts after a moment. The well-like chill flows down, freezing the intestines and heart while the head begins to blaze... The sensation is enchanting.

Herbert's Orvieto is no Proust's "madeleine," although I tend to think that if the local restaurant and trattoria owners were more literary, they could put Herbert to use the way the worthy town of Illiers-Combray has used Proust. Reading Herbert's vignettes on food, I can't help but wonder what would have happened if he'd been born in a place more conducive to epicureanism. Would his aesthetic and spiritual hunger be replaced by something more mundane? But can we really imagine him in the role of a restaurant critic?

Herbert's insatiability, his voracious appetite for the experience of the world—people, landscape, food, art—makes him an ideal traveler. For him, the perfect trip is "what the Germans call *Bildungsreise*," an educational journey during which we learn about both the world and ourselves. Reading Herbert's *Barbarian in the Garden*, *Still Life with a Bridle*, or *The Labyrinth on the Sea* is also a *Bildungsreise*. At the end of "Memories of Valois," in *Barbarian*, Herbert says, "Thanks to Sassetta I shall step into the same river, and time."

Thanks to Zbigniew Herbert, I have done the same.

MY WAR ZONE

When I was growing up war hovered somewhere in the background. I was born eight years after the Second World War ended, but for a long time, at least until the early sixties, its presence was still palpable. We lived in an apartment building that survived the fighting, though the one next to it didn't and a lot of rubble still remained. When I was very little, I heard warnings about kids finding unexploded bombs and being blown up. Soon most of the ruined buildings were bulldozed, but their underground cellars filled with bricks and debris were perfect places to play. The braver and older among us would explore them and tell hair-raising tales about skeletons and ghosts in Nazi uniforms. My friends and I used the bricks to build homes for our dolls, but when all the children on our street, boys and girls, got together, we played war. The older children assigned the younger ones the role of civilians who were supposed to elude capture. No one wanted to be a German, so we drew lots. Once you were caught, the Germans pushed you and poked you with their stick machine guns, pinned your arms behind you, yelled *"Heil Hitler,"* and threatened you with death. The make-believe was fun for older kids but scary for the little ones, who would often end up crying. Even though I soon claimed membership in the older group, my heart raced and my hands felt clammy because of how real our games were to me.

Our family members still talked about the war as if it had happened yesterday, and like many children of my generation, I developed a taste for war stories. Once I heard one, I wanted to hear it again, since each time new details emerged and repetition made it even more real. I had my favorites. I'd often ask my grandmother to tell me how she went to the country to buy food and then smuggled it into Warsaw. I loved the part about her wrapping sausage around her waist and placing a slab of bacon above it. The train reeked of smoked meat, tobacco, and moonshine, which the passengers drank to keep warm in winter and bribed the German police with. There was danger in it, but overall the story had a happy ending: Grandmother arrived home with her booty. Some other stories she told me were scary. One of them was about the time she was stopped on the street in a roundup with many other people. She was coming back from a friend's place when suddenly at both ends of the street Germans on motorcycles appeared and cut the exits off, screaming *"Hände hoch."* Trucks drove up, the captives started to be loaded into them. She knew what would happen. Some time later her family would hear of the executions. "So how did you escape?" I asked. There was this older German man, she told me, and he took pity on her when she begged him to let her go back to her children who were alone at home. He grabbed her arm and pushed her toward the door of the building they stood in front of. She opened it and ran to the end of a long hallway. A woman, maybe a janitor's wife, let her into her own apartment, where Grandmother sat shaking until it was again safe to go out on the street.

Mother had a few stories too. The war years in Warsaw, hiding in the building's basement during the German air raids in September 1939 and then during the 1944 Warsaw Uprising, had left a deep imprint on her psyche. She witnessed atrocities, knew of the Gestapo arrests of family friends and neighbors, heard of street executions. I learned from her how terrifying and chancy life was under the German occupation. Each time you left home, you risked your life, but you had to take risks because life had to go on. She talked about attending clandestine lessons, carrying her books and notebooks in a basket covered with vegetables in case a patrol stopped her. She told me how frightened she was that one of the Germans would want to poke under her wilted carrots and parsnips and that she'd get caught and shot on the spot.

Father's war experiences were on the Front. He was born in Lithuania, and when the Red Army came, even though he was Polish, he was forced to join and fought all the way to Berlin. He didn't want to tell war stories the way Grandmother did. He only once told me that the noise of machine guns and *katyushas* was deafening, and he dreamed of being in a quiet place. Much later I found out the reason for his reticence: he was a deserter from the Red Army. When the train carrying the soldiers from Berlin stopped in Poland, he escaped. Like his companions, he was convinced that the troops were being sent to fight the Japanese. Some good soul gave him civilian clothes and for a long time he lay low. So strong was his fear of repercussions that until three years before his death in 1983 he never confided in anyone.

When I started school at age six, war became alive in a different way, this time through a potent medium—the movies. On public anniversaries such as the beginning of World War II, the October Revolution or Armistice Day—called the Day of Victory—students had to convene in the auditorium where we listened to the principal's speech followed by the recitation of poems suited to the occasion with the school choir singing patriotic songs and often ending with "The International." After the so-called "official" part we would be shown a movie. These movies were sometimes feature films and sometimes documentaries about the Red Army soldiers fighting the Nazis, about the concentration camps, or the partisans and the resistance movement. I was too young to remember their titles. One movie, though, which I saw a few years later, must have deeply affected me because I recall it to this day. It was *Child of War* which tells the story of a young boy whose family is killed and who escapes from a concentration camp. He joins the army to fight because he wants revenge and refuses to go to school. I saw this movie many times. The school authorities must have decided it was a perfect tool for bringing the horrors of war home to us. I don't believe they appreciated its artistic value. Later I learned that the film was made by Andrey Tarkovsky and won the Golden Lion at the Venice Film Festival. I identified with the tragic characters from the movies we were shown and then made up my own stories in which I saved them, trying to make up for what really happened on the screen. The shared element of my stories was a qualified happy ending. I knew enough to realize that a fairy tale conclusion would be inappropriate.

I don't remember exactly when I became aware of my grandmother's preparations for the next war, but I couldn't have been older than four. She must have been doing it for years, though the fact didn't register with me until then. One day I noticed brown paper bags and burlap sacks full of flour, sugar, barley, and kasha standing under the kitchen table. When I asked her why we needed so much, she simply said "We have to be ready for war." She'd start making those purchases at the beginning of July. Since the last war had started on September

1, she somehow convinced herself that another one was bound to begin on the same day. She was guilty of magical thinking in reverse. The war didn't break out and we ate all the provisions. Then the following year, about the same time as before, Grandmother would again embark on a buying spree. She wasn't crazy. She was one of the sanest people I've ever known, yet she behaved in a completely irrational way. I had no reason to question her words. I understood that at any time war could strut onto the stage, and we had to be prepared. That procedure continued for many years until one day Grandmother decided that September 1 wouldn't be repeated.

*

In daylight I was a happy enough child, not troubled by the menace of war unless I played with other children or re-enacted some of my made up stories. The worst fears descended on me at bedtime when my imagination roamed where daylight wouldn't let it go. I worried about war cutting my life short and snatching everything I knew. I felt that I was running out of time and needed to rehearse my options. I tried striking bargains with God. I would be really good if only war could be postponed. Maybe He wouldn't start it until five years from now. How old would I be then? Or better still, maybe He'd wait ten years or even more. At least by then I could have lived a bit. I must have had little hope of surviving or perhaps I just thought that life during war wasn't the kind of life I wanted. I felt the urgency to grow up and live quickly, but I didn't know how to go about it. Would I be able to experience all of life—marry and have children—before that cataclysmic event?

I gave a lot of thought to the possibility of escape. I compiled a list of countries which were untouched by the last war. Our tomorrow was uncertain, but in Australia and the two Americas, each new day would come surely and predictably and turn quietly into yesterday. The problem was that trains couldn't take me there, and planes would be shot down. Besides, the next war might entangle the whole world. Reluctantly, I had to admit these safe places were far away and out of reach.

*

Sometime in the early 1960s nuclear war entered my consciousness. I probably heard those two words on the radio or at another school-wide assembly we had been herded into. I figured that all my worst suspicions were about to come true. I wondered if this new war would be like the last one with which I was on such intimately familiar terms. My father managed to assuage my fears somewhat when he said that after the horrors of the last world war, nobody wanted another one, not even the Russians. The Germans had now somehow disappeared as a threat. This information made enough of an impression on me to put an end to my anxious nightly ruminations. But before the specter vanished from my daily life, it had already etched itself firmly into my unconscious mind.

The irony is that I was relieved of my anxiety at the time of the Cuban Missile Crisis when the world did indeed seem on the brink of another military clash. For us in Poland it was no threat but a Soviet propaganda ploy, the Kremlin rattling its saber, and few people seriously considered the possibility of a nuclear conflict. We suspected that the Russians didn't even have nuclear weapons. When President Kennedy's gambit worked, the unanimous voice in Poland was "Didn't we tell you so?"

Years later when I already lived in the United States, I was surprised when I found out how real the possibility of a nuclear war was to people here. Many friends told me of emergency preparedness drills that they participated in at school and of their parents discussing the imminent threat of a Soviet invasion. My Mississippi-born husband remembers how all the students had to sit with their hands on top of their heads and their backs against the wall in the school's hallway. To him war was something scary but abstract. He'd heard about the Second World War, but the war that he could translate into images was the Civil War simply because its history had been drummed into his head. No wonder then that he began to expect the Soviet troops coming as a cavalry charge wearing Yankee uniforms.

I didn't know about the Vietnam War until my family bought its first television set some time in 1964. My father, who always raved about the lies in the newspapers, now added TV to a list of liars. Nevertheless, he regularly watched the evening news and regularly dismissed it as hogwash. Anti-American propaganda was nothing new in Poland, but the war must have thrown him into a moral quandary. On one hand, he saw the widespread suffering of the Vietnamese. On the other, he didn't believe the reporting and wanted his trust in the United States to remain unshaken. Maybe my inability to remember any exchanges on that topic can mean only one thing: it was never discussed at home. Since at that time I didn't watch the news, I may have seen only bits and pieces of the war footage. When the Vietnam War escalated in 1968, the events right under our noses, in Poland and then in Czechoslovakia, were too overwhelming for anyone to pay attention to what was happening in a corner of Asia. We understood that a war was raging there, but most of us knew little about it.

*

It was years before I realized how uncertain life must have felt to my parents and grandparents—how their war past and post-war experiences had contaminated their present. I didn't know at the time that they censored what they told me about the war for fear that at school I might make a negative comment about our Soviet saviors or say something equally unorthodox. And while I heard a lot of war stories, the post-war period for a long time was taboo. It wasn't until my late teens that a narrative of that part of my family members' experience began to cohere in my mind.

After the war they moved to the area of Poland that used to be East Prussia. As compensation for the territories in the East which became part of the Soviet Union, it was allotted to Poland through the post-war treaties which, unchallenged, freely shifted borders, displaced people, and destroyed whatever paltry remains of their way of life the war had left undamaged. For my family the fear of war was compounded by the fear that the previous German owners would return and demand what was theirs—their homes, buildings, farms. In case that happened, they again would have to run for their lives and leave everything behind. The respite they had hoped for at the end of the war never came. The power transfer from the Germans to the Soviet army and the Soviet security forces happened quickly. Soon after the corrupt election of 1947, which ignored the provisions of Yalta and Potsdam, Stalinism began to reign. No one felt safe. The social fabric was destroyed and normal human interactions were imbued with suspicion and distrust. At that time my grandmother owned a small grocery store in the town the family had settled in. She ran the store for a while, and the way my aunt tells it, she also ran her mouth. Since private ownership was condemned, her store was closed down, and Grandmother as an enemy of the new order was sent to a prison camp to be re-educated. She was released after a few months, maybe because she was divorced and had two underage daughters to take care of. In 1953 Stalin died, but his death changed little. They had to wait until 1956 for the "thaw" to begin. Things improved a little, yet Poland's political situation remained as precarious as ever. It's true that the country was a Soviet satellite, not one of its republics. Russia, however, could always try to turn it into one. Is it any wonder that my family members and so many others felt as if they were living on a powder keg which could explode at any moment? Czesław Miłosz captured this feeling very well when in *Native Realm* he commented that one should never be too confident going out for a walk. It's not only that something may happen to us; our home may no longer be there, and the walk may turn out to be very long. Like most survivors, my family wanted to put the war past behind them, but for the longest time it refused to let them out of its stranglehold. When it began to recede, gradually and unhurriedly, they could focus on what was at hand: the shaky ground of their present lives.

Unlike the adults, I didn't expect the ground under my feet to give at any moment. But I must have soaked up the atmosphere we lived in because I had never rid myself of the feeling that my life was provisional. Despite that sense of transience and impermanence, I did develop roots. They didn't go deep below the surface the way roots of people born in more fortunate places do since all along I was priming myself for disaster that would involve a possible departure. I tried to be one step ahead of whatever destructive tide could sweep me away. If someone asked me back then what I feared I wouldn't have been able to provide a concrete answer. It wasn't war that loomed in my imaginings; it was something indeterminate, something akin to a primal dread that cave dwellers experienced when faced with the incomprehensible and threatening world. I can't say that such feelings blighted my everyday life, but an undercurrent of fatalism simmered somewhere within me. While I formed deep attachments to people and have always been good at cultivating friendships—even those that go back to my childhood—my attachment to places bore the telltale signs of doomed love. It was like falling in love and knowing from the start that the relationship would soon end and I'd be left heartbroken and hurt. Place was important, and the ideal was to remain where one was born and where one's family had lived for generations, but I knew by my grand-parents' and parents' example that this was rarely feasible in a country of redrawn borders, deportations, expatriations, migrations, all engendered by historical upheavals of one kind or another.

*

My immigration to America wasn't caused by economic or political reasons or even by my hankering for stability. Many people of my generation had been leaving Poland for years, but I never planned to emigrate. I did it because I met an American and married him. When I came here, I came to the country that in my childhood imaginings symbolized solidity, predictability, and safety. Those fantasies were based on what I had overheard the adults say. The Soviet Union was the beast that wanted to devour us, and the United States was the only country that could stand up to it. America was like all those brave sheriffs from the westerns my dad and I regularly went to see in our local movie theater. Even politically savvy people had this naïve belief in the United States coming to our rescue should the neighbor to the east misbehave. The country's luke-warm reaction to the Warsaw Pact invasion of Czechoslovakia in 1968 should have been a sobering blow, but it did little to undermine that belief. In our uncertain situation denial was a saving grace. We had to have faith in the existence of some force for good.

For many people immigration means an escape from the uncertainty of today, and at the time of my arrival in the US right after the suspension of martial law, it must have to some extent signified the same thing for me. But as they say, you get what you wish for. The fickle Spiritus Mundi decided to grant me my wishes, but couldn't resist playing a trick on me. While I could stop worrying about the possibility of the Soviet invasion or the communist government's next move, my sense of life as provisional and unreal didn't abate. As it started to feed on the dichotomies of an immigrant's experience, it got a second wind. You crave stability and end up in another betwixt-and-between place. You yearn to be anchored but feel you've lost your bearings. Your personal life may be happy and stable, and yet you have a sense that it's not quite real, that you're living a script that was written for someone else. It was a long while before my life here stopped seeming like suspended time, like a vacation from which sooner or later I'd have to return. It was impossible to convey my feelings to my American friends. To them I should be happy as someone who managed to escape, even though they knew that my arrival here wasn't an escape. When I tried to explain my mental and emotional state, they would give me a sympathetic but perplexed look. I must have seemed like one of those neurotic, obsessive, and melancholy Eastern Europeans who don't know how lucky they are to be in a free country where the monsters of the past rarely rear their heads.

*

I lived in America when the end of the Cold War was loudly proclaimed and followed by the declaration that we had arrived at the end of history. Together with my compatriots I shared the joy and exultation at the downfall of communism, but like most of them I was skeptical about the optimistic assessments that we had managed to outwit history and that the world was at last close to a utopia, when there would be fewer conflicts and in due time peace would reign. Soon after, the first Gulf War began, and history caught up with us. It entered our family living room through the detailed daily coverage on CNN. At that point my childhood fears had long been erased, even though now and then war still haunted me in my dreams. The Gulf War, maybe because of its distance and the nature of the reporting on it, had for me the aura of a fictitious event. When it was over, it was easily forgotten as things that don't have a direct impact on us tend to be forgotten. Then came the wars in the Balkans, so much closer to where I used to live than the Middle East, and they revived Eastern Europeans' fears of the conflict escalating into another world war. While I dutifully perused newspaper accounts of the developments over there, I didn't succumb to those fears. I was relieved, selfishly, that I was safely ensconced in my predictable America.

On September 11 I had the first inkling that something was seriously amiss when I went to work at the college where I taught and saw stone-faced students staring at a large TV screen. Later that morning I learned the full extent of what had happened.

For the longest time I feared that those attacks were a preamble to further horrors. Even when they didn't materialize, each day that our daughters went to school, I was sick with worry about their safety. I shared in the pervasive feeling of disbelief that such attacks could have taken place at all. Whereas in my former life, from childhood on, I was trained to expect the worst, I now lived in an optimistic, forward-looking country, in which bad things weren't supposed to happen. And yet, they did happen. I was shocked as if a promise that I'd been given and counted on was desultorily withdrawn. Somewhere within, however, a voice kept whispering: Shouldn't you have known better? How could you have been so naïve as to think that any place could be spared?

*

Today, years after September 11, the date that for my American neighbors has acquired the mythical meaning that September 1 held for my grandmother and people of her generation, the conviction that the United States would be immune to the woes of the world at large hasn't returned. The wind of history may not blow here with as much force as in other parts of the world, but it has reached the country's shores. If I were a child now, I wouldn't be able to imagine an ideal shelter for myself where I could hide from the world's madness, the way I did growing up in Poland. In truth, what child today could compile a list of safe places? Today's children can dream only of a place which would perhaps be less unsafe than the war zone in which they happen to live.

OBJECTS OF AFFECTION

Each summer when I'm in Krakow, I make weekly trips to a flea market close to our apartment. This particular market also sells antiques, but it doesn't aspire to a more lofty name because it also peddles secondhand books, last year's issues of fashion magazines, handmade jewelry, items that aren't old in the sense that antiques are supposed to be. A valuable nineteenth-century chest of drawers or a gilded mirror enjoys good neighborly relations with an electric coffee grinder and rusty door handles. It would probably be easier to attempt a list of things that aren't sold there than the ones that are. If someone is looking for a rare item, his friends will invariably suggest going to the flea market. When I was looking for a desk, I first went there and bought a beautiful Art Nouveau table which recovered its former looks after being renovated. I love the market because I love rummaging through old things and because I usually will find something that I absolutely want to have. I love running my fingers over the shapely back of a violin, tracing the grooves in a century-old high back chair, or gently tapping a porcelain cup to hear it tinkle. I know that to some people viewing old objects with something akin to reverence is a silly affectation. But particularly there, in a country that wasn't spared violent entanglements with History, an old photograph, a water pitcher, a clock that stood on someone's mantelpiece and was miraculously salvaged from a bombed-out building—those mute witnesses to human life inspire awe and amazement at the mere fact of their survival. They connect us to the past and its messy materiality by making that past more concrete, more tangible. In them we see the reflected wisdom of our simple human order.

*

I was a child of the fifties, growing up in a communist country beset by shortages of practically everything—food, clothes, furniture—and that circumstance may have been responsible for my complicated attitude toward objects. We had few toys or books, and we mostly wore hand-me-downs. A pair of mittens, a teddy bear, and a chocolate bar for Christmas were enough. Once in a while we also got skates, bikes, musical instruments. "Abundance" had no place in our vocabulary and in our world, but we were happy with what we had the way that only children can be. We were unaware that our lives were in any way circumscribed, although the reality we lived in trained us early on that there was a huge gap between wanting something and getting it. After all, even people with money had to hustle and resort to underhanded maneuvers, including bribery, to buy things.

For many years I had only one doll, which my father somehow managed to procure when I was four years old.

Made in Germany, Gabriela had two long braids. She was a beautiful doll, not like the ones sold in toy stores, and though I had other dolls later, she remained special. When the mechanism responsible for her making a crying sound broke, we took her to the doll clinic. At that time nothing was thrown away if there was even a slight chance that it could be repaired. I had Gabriela until I turned fourteen when, in a grown-up gesture, I bequeathed her to a young cousin.

By the time I graduated from high school I was a person of substance, or so I thought. The shortages never disappeared, but it was easier to get things. I had a Chinese fountain pen and two ball point pens which I kept in my desk drawer and would only use at home. I boasted several records that my sister and I listened to on a gramophone she had been given as a name-day present a few years before. Some of them were by the popular Polish rock bands, and one was Beethoven's Fifth Symphony, the only classical music record I had for a long time. I listened to it so often that to this day I can hum the whole piece from beginning to end. I also had a bookcase with a sliding glass front that was filled with books. I was very possessive of the books I owned and only reluctantly loaned them to friends. When my younger sister took one out, I insisted she put it back in the exact same spot.

My possessiveness may have had a lot to do with how difficult books were to come by. They were published in small numbers, and there was such a huge demand for them among the intelligentsia that the good ones disappeared from stores very quickly. On my way back from school I often made a detour and walked by the local bookstore to look at the window where new arrivals would be displayed. That was how I spotted a four-volume *War and Peace* which cost eighty złoty, not a negligible sum. I had only thirty. The clerk told me this was the only copy in the store. I knew the book would be sold soon so I decided to go to my father's office and beg him for a loan, which he gave me at once. Clutching the money, I ran back to the bookstore, breathless and worried that the book would no longer be there. I realize that what I'm saying must seem pathetic to a person raised in the comforts of a free market economy where it's enough to think of something to find it immediately in the store.

It might sound more poignant if I said that books and records helped me escape the surrounding grayness and drabness and that my hunting for them wasn't solely motivated by my newly developed acquisitiveness or a collector's instinct. But if I said that, I'd be practicing revisionist history. The truth is that we didn't see the grayness and drabness—not yet. This realization came much later. So if it was aesthetic escapism, it was the universal kind, not fueled by our peculiar political circumstances.

My youthful materialism thrived in a country where materialism—unless of the Marxist variety—was unanimously condemned as the ugly outgrowth of western consumer societies. We knew this was just an ideological cover-up for the never-ending shortages. My brand of materialism didn't belong in a consumer society, either, because it was a kind of disproportionate attachment to things that was caused by scarcity, something unheard of in a market economy. I couldn't want more, new, or better. Such wanting was at best a futile and abstract exercise, so I learned to practice self-limitation. Paradoxically, however, I knew what I liked and wanted, and would have had no trouble making a choice had I been given the chance. When you're faced with overabundance, assaulted by things and more things, it's often difficult to say what you like or want, but that at least wasn't our problem. I don't mean to praise privation or claim that we were somehow better or more virtuous than people who inhabited a consumer heaven and whose wishes could be automatically fulfilled. I'm only saying that my relationship to things was developed under a different set of circumstances. I did care about possessions, no question about that. I wanted to hang on to what I had, and now and then add to my stock if I came across the right item. More often than not chance ruled my acquisitions. I had to sift through what was available in the hopes of finding something special among a slew of worthless objects. That was also true of buying the so-called practical items. I might have been walking by a shoe store when I spotted a delivery truck. That sight was enough to make me stand in line. If I was lucky, I might have ended up buying a pair of sneakers. I might have also wasted my time because I liked none of the shoes or couldn't get my size. People would often buy things they didn't need or want, just in case. You could never tell when they might come in handy or be used to barter.

*

I came to America for an academic exchange program. That wasn't my first visit to a western country. In previous years I'd spent some time in England, Germany, and a semester in Florida at the invitation of a Fulbright professor who taught at my university, and I'd already seen stores overflowing with goods I didn't know existed. But in 1984, three years after brutal martial law that obliterated any hope for change, Poland experienced unprecedented shortages as if the communist government was doing everything in its power to punish the recalcitrant populace. To buy meat we needed coupons, and the same was true of sugar. Chocolate was rationed too, but you had to have children to get it. Grocery stores had shelves stacked only with vinegar and low quality tea, called *Popularna*—Popular, the irony of whose name wasn't lost on us. Other necessities were so hard to get that serpentine lines formed in front of the stores before daylight.

A few days after I arrived in the United States a friend took me to a supermarket on Long Island where she lived. I knew what to expect, but as I kept watching people piling item after item into their shopping carts until they looked like elaborate pyramids, I felt sick. Who needs so much food, I thought. This was almost obscene. Soon my own shopping habits had changed and begun to resemble the American ones—if not in quantity then in the way I went about buying.

But for many years I didn't quite shed my old ways. For one thing, I attempted to have all broken items repaired. I remember insisting that my husband take me to a repair shop to have a strap re-attached to a sandal that I'd bought a month before. The sandals were cheap, I couldn't have paid more than $20 for them. To my dismay I discovered that fixing the shoe would have cost me more than half that price. I gradually learned the same was true of electronics and many other items of daily use.

My reluctance to part with something that could possibly be repaired, which against my better judgment I still exhibit, comes from my grandmother. I can also attribute to her my preference for well-made objects with a long life span ahead of them. I remember how she often said that she couldn't afford poor quality. By today's standards she had few clothes, and she wore her coats, hats, and jackets for many long years. All her clothes were made to last, carefully sewn of good quality fabrics by a seamstress or a tailor. The same can be said about her shoes. She only had four pairs of them, a pair for each season, spring and fall counting as one, and one pair of "going out" shoes that she'd wear to name-day parties or family celebrations. She dutifully carried them to a shoe repair shop if any of them needed new soles, straps or buckles. Her apartment was furnished in what I came to call utilitarian style: the necessary items, simple and functional, no bric-a-brac, no trinkets of any kind. The only older object in her place was an antique napkin holder, with a marble bottom and brass top whose origin I know nothing about. She must have developed this unsentimental attitude after everything she owned perished in the burning of her apartment building during the 1944 Warsaw Uprising.

After many days of hiding in the building's basement and the subsequent defeat of the Uprising, she was taken to a camp in Pruszków with my aunt who was barely a year old, and my mother, eleven at the time. My grandfather had disappeared at the beginning of the turmoil and found his wife and daughters much later. She had a baby carriage, a suitcase with a change of clothes, a handful of photos, and a silver sugar bowl that at the last minute she snatched off the table. I never thought to ask her about the sugar bowl, although I wondered why she took it. Besides the photos, that was the only item that had nothing to do with survival. I can see her hurriedly packing clothes, a mug, a spoon, a blanket for the baby to keep her warm in the basement. For a moment her eyes rest on the silver sugar bowl on the kitchen table, a wedding gift from her husband's aunt. She hesitates, then quickly wraps it in her daughter's blouse and puts it in the suitcase. Did she want to keep at least one thing from her apartment as a reminder of the life which she knew was about to end? Or did she just grab it thinking she might swap it for food or use it to bribe a German soldier?

Eventually, she ended up living for several months with a peasant family near Łowicz. They treated the survivors from Warsaw like their own kin, and Grandmother gave them the sugar bowl, the only thing she could give to repay their kindness. When Warsaw was freed by the Red Army, she returned, hoping that maybe her building was still there. She saw only its skeleton and her beloved city in ruins. Then and there she decided the family had to move elsewhere. They went to the former East Prussia, labeled the Recovered Territories, and settled in a small town which was relatively unscathed by the war. Though there were ruins from bombed buildings there, the majority of the apartment buildings and one-family houses remained intact. Their former German owners fled in panic from the advancing Red Army. To save their lives they had to lose everything, abandon all the possessions they had accumulated over the years, just like Grandmother, who had to leave her apartment and all it contained. The difference was that none of her possessions survived while here the newly arrived, shipwrecked people took up residence in apartments that were furnished, had pots and pans, rugs, bedclothes, pictures and all sorts of knick knacks.

I often wondered how my grandmother felt in a strange apartment where the smells of the previous owners still wafted in the air and the sheets were still warm from their bodies. Among strange furniture, salt shakers with the inscription *Salz*, faucets with Gothic script, she must have felt like an intruder. She missed her Warsaw apartment that she had patiently and lovingly decorated. Now she had nothing of her own, no objects imbued with memories, nothing to fill out the space and make it hers. She never felt comfortable surrounded by all those strange things, that post-German stuff as we came to call everything that had remained after the German exodus. She also sensed the wrongness of her situation, its moral illegality, even though it was done with official encouragement and approval. Contrary to the official propaganda, there was nothing she could recover in those "Recovered Territories."

When I was about ten, Grandmother moved into her own small house on the outskirts of town. She took with her the furniture that was in the apartment because that's what she had. She couldn't have just sold it and bought new items. To begin with, she didn't have the money, but even if she did, the rampant shortages of everything would have made buying new items difficult. She lived in that house for less than two years and hated the distance she had to walk to get to town.

When she sold the house, this time she sold it with everything in it, and got a studio in a newly built apartment building that had the telltale look of communist style residential architecture. She was relieved to get rid of all the post-German objects she'd never considered hers. Because her new place was tiny, she needed only a few items to furnish it. Those post-German items were more attractive and better made than what she had bought, but at last she had things that belonged to her. And once she furnished her place, she never replaced anything in it, and she lived to be ninety-three. Her furniture and all her other possessions were functional and practical, and that was all she cared about.

*

Grandmother died in the fall of 2001. Mother was no longer alive, so the task of dismantling Grandmother's apartment fell to my aunt. I told her I'd like to get something that belonged to my grandmother, a keepsake. My aunt was at a loss because Grandmother had none of the items that family members usually keep after a person's death. I ended up with a round glass paperweight and some photos. My aunt took the napkin holder and my sister a metal basket for keeping needles, receipts, and small change. Was the paperweight an object full of memories for me? Not really. I knew that it was hers and that it was in her apartment, but it wasn't like those things that overwhelm us with nostalgia when we hold them or look at them. I have a lot of memories attached to Grandmother's apartment, the many times I visited her, the meals she cooked for me in her cramped kitchen, and I know that these memories are more important than a trinket I could have inherited. But sometimes I do wish she had left behind some things she valued and loved which I could keep now and then pass on to my daughters. My grandmother is still alive in my memories.

My daughters' memories are limited as we could visit her only in the summer. When I'm gone, she'll die a second death. An object that belonged to her could then serve as a reminder of her life, a souvenir connecting generations.

When I came to America, I left behind everything I owned in Poland. I arrived with a large backpack and a suitcase the size of a larger carry-on, which contained my clothes and a few books. In this sense my situation was like my grandmother's, but there the resemblance ends. My circumstances weren't the result of a war or a historical upheaval. Yes, I did lose things I was attached to, though they didn't just disappear. They simply changed owners, and most of them remained in the family. And unlike my grandmother, I felt I needed things for my emotional well-being. My future husband had a lot of books and records, all of which I happily adopted as mine. Gradually, we filled our house with more books and records, more photos and photo albums, china, pictures, artwork, Christmas decorations. Some years later our daughters' dolls, teddy bears, drawings, seashells, rocks, homework and school projects were added to the trove of important objects. I'm not a hoarder, but I'm sentimental about things.

My attachment to objects was put to a test in 2009 when we made a cross-country move from California to Massachusetts. We knew we had to get rid of a lot of stuff. I decided to pack most of our belongings myself, separating the items of value from the ones relegated to the giveaway pile. The process was lengthy, and it exasperated my husband who has a very down-to-earth, no-nonsense attitude toward possessions. He urged me to throw things away since most of what I wanted to save I would never use or even look at. But with many objects I felt as if I had opened a sluice gate: I was flooded by memories. And once that happened, I knew I had to keep those items, no matter how trifling they would seem to someone else. I kept my daughters' newborn caps, their christening gowns, their first diaries with lockets, the cards they wrote to me on Mother's Day. I kept some pictures, vases, plates, table runners I got from different relatives in Poland, even though I knew they would stay in the attic until the next inventory. And against my husband's advice to toss them, I even salvaged some items that he had as a child, like two model tractors he received at age five from the Delta Implement Company in Indianola, Mississippi, and that now adorn the top of the bookshelf in his study. Will our daughters hang on to these things when the time comes to dismantle our house? I have no way of knowing. I do suspect, though, that they will want to keep our collection of books with its many first editions, the artwork, the photo albums, my mother's and my jewelry, a few antiques we have, and the Polish stoneware that I've been collecting for years. Maybe they will even keep some of the things that my husband wanted condemned to the junk pile. Maybe they'll be grateful to things for the delight they give us and the lessons they teach about the triumph and defeat of mortal matter.

*

Some years ago, in a world literature class, I was teaching Tadeusz Borowski's *This Way for the Gas, Ladies and Gentlemen*. One story in the collection, "The Man with the Package," a mere four pages long, provoked a very lively exchange. The story's main character is a Jew who has the position of a Schreiber in Birkenau's hospital, a position that for a long time offers him protection other prisoners don't have. Besides clerical work, his duties involve accompanying Jews selected for the gas chamber to the wash room, from which they are taken to the crematoria. One day the Schreiber himself comes down with the flu and is selected for the gas. On his way there he carries a cardboard box tied with a string; the box contains a pair of boots, a spoon, a knife, and a few other items. Seeing this, the story's narrator says: "He could show a little more good sense. . . . He knows perfectly well   that within an hour or two he will go to the gas chamber, naked without his shirt, and without his package. What an extraordinary attachment to the last bit of property!" Just like the narrator, my students found the Schreiber's behavior bizarre. They couldn't understand why, when faced with imminent death, he would hang on to what were to them worthless things. They hadn't yet learned that objects help exorcise some of our fears, that they are stronger than we are, perfect and independent, that they can give us a semblance of permanence and grant a stay against chaos, darkness, oblivion.

OUR DAILY DRINK

THE REAL THING

I have a long history with tea because I started drinking it as a child. Back then it could easily be called our ethnic drink. It was served to young children as often as milk, but only with certain foods since a lot of people, among them my family, believed that milk didn't go with meat dishes, cold cuts, or fish—an effect of the large Jewish population in prewar Poland with its kosher rules. I have to admit that when I first went to the United States and saw people eating steak accompanied by a glass of milk I was shocked by the wrongness of that combination.

The tea given to kids wasn't herbal, although such teas were widely available, Poland having a long tradition of natural medicine. Herbal teas were used for minor ailments, like mint for stomach upsets, sage for sore throat, or linden flowers for colds. Babies would get chamomile and fennel for colic and better digestion, but once they were out of diapers, they got the real thing, and that's what they drank with their meals. In the spring and summer there was fizzy water with orange or lemon flavor, called orangeade or lemonade. It was a treat, something special, bought only on outings to the park or school trips, not a daily drink like soda in the United States. Adults would often drink mineral water that came from many of Poland's mineral springs, but to children it tasted bland, and some of it had a sulfurous aftertaste.

At that time no one paid attention to the caffeine content, or maybe people just were unaware of it. I suspect, though, that even if someone had told them, they wouldn't have cared. Children had to drink something, so hot tea was served year round, on sultry summer days and during freezing winters. I never found it strange, either, until many years later, in the mid-seventies, when an American friend living in Poland expressed surprise that tea was given to four-year olds instead of fruit juice. "It has *caffeine*," he said. Well, it did, but fruit juice wasn't popular for many reasons. It only came in small bottles, not in half-gallon cartons or gallon-sized jars like American orange juice, and it was expensive. It was also thick and, to a child, it tasted awful.

THE THRILL OF IT ALL

When I was in high school Polish television began showing American comedies with Doris Day. The censors must have decided that there was nothing incendiary in the adventures of an American housewife, nothing that would divert us from our attachment to socialism. After all, none of us wanted the glories of the life of a stay-at-home mom. We were no longer bombarded with posters of women on tractors the way our mothers were, but we all planned to have jobs as teachers, doctors, engineers. So the censors were right in that respect. But they didn't foresee the impact of one small element we saw in those movies that to me and my friends became the symbol of glamorous American life.

The characters in the movies always drank orange juice with breakfast. And that orange juice connoted all the comforts and sophistication of life in the West. No one in Poland could drink orange juice like that since oranges were only available once a year, at Christmas. They were small, rarely sweet, and involved standing in long lines. It wouldn't occur to anyone to squeeze the juice of such an expensive fruit. Besides, who owned a juicer? When juicers did at last show up, people used them to make carrot or apple juice for babies.

During my visit to the US in 1975, I stayed with an American family where the father would take a can of frozen orange pulp and turn it into a pitcher of juice. I watched this miracle many times and happily drank the juice. I thought I was partaking in and immersing myself in genuine American life. After the obligatory orange juice, my hosts drank coffee with breakfast, but I stuck to my Polish habits and to tea. On the few occasions I had coffee, I found it thoroughly unimpressive.

ESSENCE

We drank tea because we had few other options. Should anyone be concerned with the amount of caffeine Polish children absorbed on a daily basis, I hasten to explain that the tea was weak and would never satisfy a gourmet. It was copiously sweetened with sugar and, during inclement weather, with raspberry syrup to ward off colds—provided that the mother or grandmother of the family had devoted some time over the summer to making preserves, syrups, and pickles. A slice of lemon would appear in the tea whenever a family member was lucky enough to have bought them. Milk could also be added, and then it was called "bawarka," the name referring to the way Bavarian princes drank their tea.

Another reason for the weakness of the tea was economic. Times were hard and people tried to cut corners and save wherever possible, even on tea. It was prepared in a different way than in England or in America. Our teapots were small and served for brewing *esencja*, or tea essence, which as the name suggests was thick and strong. A little bit of it was poured into mugs, cups, or even more often into clear glasses (a custom that came to Poland from Russia in the nineteenth century), and then hot water was added. Children got very little of the *esencja*, which would be dispensed throughout the day. When it was all gone, the same tea leaves were often used again by pouring boiling water on them. The second time around, the tea had none of the aroma or flavor of the first brew, but it saved money and time.

OOLONG VS. YUNNAN

The cheapest tea was Oolung, and it didn't boast a lot of flavor, but that was what we drank on a daily basis. A bit more expensive Madras had better taste, although I'm sure it wouldn't have satisfied tea connoisseurs. During those times, the authorities didn't spoil us with any form of luxury. When someone wanted to crack a joke about the poor quality of the tea, they'd say that the people's republics got the tea leaves that were swept off the warehouse floor after the real tea was shipped to the wealthier western countries.

In the late sixties, as far as I remember, yet another kind of tea showed up in the stores: Yunnan, the queen of all teas, even though its package was as shoddy as those of the lower-class teas. Yunnan had amazing taste and flavor. I first drank it in college. As students we rarely bothered to brew tea the way our families did at home. We would simply place two heaping teaspoons of tea leaves in a glass or mug and pour boiling water on top. Once the leaves fell to the bottom, it was ready. You just had to be careful not to stir it if you didn't want to end up with a mouthful of tea leaves. This tea was so strong it could knock you off your feet, and few students drank it with sugar, which was for the unsophisticated sissies. I remember drinking cup after cup while sitting in my friends' dorm room. I should also add that at that time most people made coffee the same fashion because almost no one owned a coffee maker. And coffee grinds could find their way into your mouth, too. That often happened to unsuspecting foreigners. Cafés had large espresso machines, and in big cities they were put to use. In most other places they just sat on the counters like oversized decorations. It was easier for the employees to just put ground coffee into a cup than have to clean the espresso maker. If a customer insisted, the waitress would give him a dirty look.

THIS IS IT!

When Edward Gierek, the new Communist Party secretary, came to power in 1970 after a round of strikes, he let us pretend that we had transcended barnyard socialism and would at last be able to buy what people in the West had access to for years. This was when Pepsi and Coca Cola were introduced in Poland, an obvious sign of progress since in the 1950s Coca Cola was condemned as a corrupt American drink and compared to the potato bug that the Americans were accused of dropping over Eastern Europe to destroy the crops of the valiant communist countries. Earlier, the two sodas could only be bought with western money at the Pewex—popularly called the dollar store—which was out of bounds for most of the population that had no foreign currency.

While in the US Pepsi and Coke were everyday drinks, in Poland they carried the connotation of western luxury. A bottle of one of these legendary liquids wasn't cheap, but who could resist their mystique? Since the Pepsi and Coca Cola companies vied for their spheres of influence in Poland, to forestall wicked capitalist competition the communist government decided to divide Poland into the Pepsi and Coke regions. In practical terms, this meant that either one or the other of the sodas was available in any given city, and for quite a while, until their production in Poland met the demand, the coveted beverage only reached big cities. In a country of permanent shortages there was little or no advertising, but I remember a competition for the most catchy advertising slogan for Coke. The one that took the prize was quite simple: *Coca Cola: this is it!*

Wrocław, where I lived, was Pepsi territory, and like many of my friends, for some time I succumbed to its lure. Most of us never really developed a taste for it, but sitting in a café and slowly sipping Pepsi gave us a feeling of refinement and worldliness. We weren't necessarily in Beverly Hills, but we'd come a long way.

If memory serves me right, I had my first Coke in Warsaw when I went there to visit a high school friend. She lived in a dorm and bought a bottle of Coke to accompany the cake that her mother had sent from home. The Coke seemed too sweet to go with the cake, but we both drank it dutifully, pouring small measures into little glasses, and when we had emptied the bottle, we immediately made tea.

Suddenly, stores also had other amazing goods like canned pineapple, crackers, and better quality tea than we used to drink and called "the straw from Mao Tse Tung's mattress." Even Yunnan, our favorite, couldn't compare with Twinings' Earl Grey, which was much more expensive and available loose or in teabags. Today I prefer loose tea leaves, but back then I'd buy Twinings in teabags, because that seemed more civilized than what I was used to. As with Pepsi and Coke, drinking this fancy tea allowed us to imagine that we were only a step away from Europe.

At the time Poland's imports from China included reasonably priced porcelain. A lot of my friends and I gave up the glasses we used to drink tea in for these delicate Chinese cups, relishing the political flavor of that decision, and ignoring the fact that the clear glasses had come to Poland from Russia long before the October revolution. The fact that China was a communist country didn't bother us one bit. After all, it was far away.

THE ENGLISH WAY

In 1973, I went to England, my first western country. I worked as a waitress at a restaurant in Norfolk where I learned to serve tea the English style, in a teapot, very strong and with milk. I was surprised to see that the milk was supposed to be poured into a cup first and then tea would be added, not the way we made our Bavarian tea. When I asked the manager about it, she told me that adding milk to the tea like we did in Poland changed its taste. I accepted that explanation without ever bothering to test the two methods to see if it was really different. Weren't the English supposed to be experts in tea drinking with a long tradition that went back to their famous tea houses? I learned to drink tea the English way and decided to try it on my family when I returned home. They politely drank it like that at first but soon reverted to their old ways, although I kept offering it to them during the weeks before going back to college.

I graduated in 1976 and got a job at my alma mater's English department. By then it was easy to buy a variety of tea in Polish stores, not just the three kinds that were available earlier. There was a choice of teas imported from England, and a relatively wide selection that came to us from the brotherly Republic of China. We could also purchase Indian tea.

Since my academic teacher's salary was pitifully low, and I could never save enough money to travel in a western country, like many of my compatriots I headed west to try to earn real money. Berlin became my place of choice, or, to be quite exact, West Berlin (the inclusion of the word "West" a practice imposed by the Communist governments to differentiate it from the "real" Berlin, the capital of the German Democratic Republic). The advantage of West Berlin lay in its closeness to Wrocław. It was also relatively easy to get a job there, illegally of course. I went to West Berlin three summers in a row and each time was fortunate enough to find employment.

I worked in a restaurant, in a café; I cleaned people's houses, and once I cleaned the apartment of an American military officer, who paid me very well and gave me a half-gallon bottle of bourbon as a parting gift. I didn't like its taste, but my male friends were overjoyed to try something so exotic. I saved my money for higher-level purposes like travel and books, yet each time, right before going back to Poland, I splurged and bought good quality tea, coffee, chocolate, and green-apple shampoo whose smell I loved.

THE OASIS OF CIVILIZATION

While in the mid-seventies you could still buy all the basic necessities in Polish stores, as time went on the shortages worsened. In 1980, the year of Solidarity's ascendance, fewer and fewer goods graced the shelves, and we had food coupons to buy meat and sugar. On my last trip to Berlin in the summer of 1981, I bought items that were no longer in the category of frills. I bought tea, too, but this time I bought it not because I wanted something more exotic that I couldn't get in Poland. I bought a lot of plain Ceylon tea because the only tea in Polish grocery stores was the undrinkable *Popularna*.

Even though it was a challenge to buy food and feed one's family, it was an exhilarating time politically, a time of hope, to which martial law put an end. All cultural events were canceled, curfew started at 10 pm, and the only thing to do was to gather at friends' apartments, drinking tea. If someone wanted something stronger, he or she would have to resort to homebrew since all the liquor stores had been closed. A lot of people started making their own liquor from sugar or anything else they had on hand in makeshift home distilleries in which the tea kettle played a major role. Besides *samizdat* publications and illegal gatherings, it was another form of defying the military government, something that even politically passive people engaged in. The adage that necessity is the mother of invention was once again proven true. Fortunately, the government couldn't forgo the revenue it got from vodka sales, so sales of liquor resumed pretty quickly. The only restriction placed on it was that stores could sell alcohol only after 1 pm, by which time one could see a line of thirsty citizens waiting for the hour of release from enforced sobriety.

Though a lot of us already had coffee makers—they made their appearance during the heyday of Gierek's rule as the first secretary—there was almost no coffee to be had. Now and then a store would get a small supply, and though the coffee was bad, a line would immediately form. Coffee aficionados, just like tea lovers, had a hard time. Despite all these shortages, the supply of Pepsi and Coke was unaffected, but few people sought to satisfy their caffeine cravings with them. If they missed the opportunity to join a line for coffee, their only hope was a café, which particularly in big cities remained an oasis of civilization. Wrocław had many good ones, and I would often take a longer route to the tram stop just to give myself an opportunity to go to the café at the Monopol Hotel where some famous and infamous people like Pablo Picasso and Adolf Hitler had stayed, and where the Polish director Andrzej Wajda filmed many scenes of his classic movie *Ashes and Diamonds*. Like most people I didn't go there for its celebrity status, but for what we called its prewar atmosphere, the highest praise that could be lavished on anything. We used the term *prewar* to refer to those amazing times when Poland wasn't part of the Soviet camp, when everything was normal, and when good quality was the norm. No one questioned the validity of that label as in our dismal state it was easier to focus on the positives and ignore the negatives of prewar Poland. In the afternoon the café was always full and filled with clouds of cigarette smoke. It was acceptable to ask people sitting at a table if it was all right to join them, provided there was an unoccupied chair. Even if the café was crowded, the answer was always yes, so I could count on finding a seat. I don't know how today I would judge the coffee served there, but back then it seemed very good. The café also had delicious cakes—excellent layer cakes—which everyone appreciated when sugar was rationed and butter had to be hunted like game.

BUCKETS

In 1984 I came to the United States. Since I'd visited America before, one of my new culture shocks was not the sheer abundance of available products, but the size of the cups people drank from and the fact that they drank while walking or driving. Either I hadn't noticed this before, I told myself, or it had been different nine years earlier. How could they enjoy their drinks on the go? Was it the outgrowth of their belief in efficiency and their reluctance to waste time? Life here was fast-paced, energetic and busy, unlike in Poland, where we took our time and drank tea or coffee sitting down and talking for hours enveloped in the atmosphere of ease and leisure.

I didn't like the plastic cups. I thought they made the drink taste funny. My future husband, Steve, had several giant ones into which he poured sodas or iced tea. They all had logos on them, like *Ole Miss* or *the Atlanta Braves*, and must have held at least 32 ounces. To me they looked like buckets. I couldn't understand why anyone would need that much liquid. His favorite soda was Diet Dr. Pepper, which my taste buds found syrupy and strange. Now and then he also drank Pepsi and Coke, but I was at least familiar with them. I couldn't believe the variety of available sodas and their great popularity. I never took to them, and even Pepsi and Coke soon lost their legendary appeal.

I remained a tea drinker but gradually converted to coffee in the morning. Steve drank coffee that came from Mr. Coffee, and it was so weak that I called it "muddy water." After a while I got him to make it stronger. I was dismayed at the poor quality of the coffee that was sold in convenience stores, off the interstate and in restaurants. I'm not talking about the high end places we couldn't afford. The tea was equally bad, served in a mug filled with lukewarm water, the flavor resembling the low quality Oolung from my childhood. Coming from a country in Eastern Europe may not have turned me into an overall gourmet, but I thought at least I knew what tea and coffee were supposed to taste like.

NATIVE WAYS

Now when I return to Poland, twenty-eight years after the ouster of communism, I can drink the same beverages that are available to me in the US. If I want to, I can buy American soft drinks or their local equivalents that taste almost the same. The store shelves are full of several brands of orange juice and other fruit juices—some of them, like blackberry or black currant, reflecting a local preference. My coffee may come from Guatemala or Costa Rica, and it may be roasted in Germany or France. Polish cafés now serve cappuccinos, unheard of before, unless someone traveled to Italy, and lattes have also gained popularity, whereas when I was growing up, the only choice was to have one's coffee black or with cream. Local habits still prevail in the way coffee is prepared. Each cup is individually brewed under pressure, and an espresso differs from it only in size. The cups are still small like they used to be, and there are only two possibilities: a four- or an eight-ounce cup, the first type referred to as small and the other as large, nothing like small, medium, and large sizes in American cafes. No one has heard of free refills, either. If you ask for white coffee, the milk is always heated and served on the side. Coffee concoctions like Frappuccinos haven't become popular yet, maybe because they would be too sweet for an average Polish person, but if they get modified to suit the local taste, they may start appearing on cafés' menus. Certain cafés in Polish malls now serve coffee and tea in paper cups, and young people walk with cups in their hands, like the residents of New York City or Tokyo. But while more and more Polish people drink coffee with their breakfast, tea continues to hold its place, and one still hears friends inviting each other to drop by for a cup. Tea comes in countless varieties and flavors and occupies its own long and high shelf in supermarkets. Even my old favorite, Yunnan, is there, but it has a new, more elegant, glossy package. Although people still cling to some of their native ways in preparing and serving their drinks, there's no denying that our drinks and drinking habits have been globalized.

Those who cringe at globalization should be reminded that tea and coffee, since they can't be cultivated everywhere, have in a sense always been global. So I don't worry about our drinks being globalized as long as our customs and traditions aren't eroded and we ourselves remain unaffected. Drinking Coke, green tea, or cappuccino won't turn us into others and make us lose our ethnic identity. Even if we now drink what the rest of the world does, we're not what we drink and never were.

MY MADELEINE

Over the years my beverage repertoire has expanded. I now enjoy red and green tea, and often buy gourmet brands at specialty stores. But I also continue bringing Yunnan from Poland since it alone still tastes the way Yunnan should.

Nowhere else have I been able to find the exact replica of the tea I used to drink in the past. I realize of course that besides its unique taste I search for something else. I want it to be my madeleine. I want it to take me on a nostalgic journey to the small room I rented on the sixth floor of an ugly high-rise, to the Odra River on whose banks I walked countless times, to the sound of my heels clicking on the cobblestone streets near the Market Square, to Wrocław where I lived so long ago.

QUINCE *Bless thee, Bottom, bless thee! Thou art translated.*
—William Shakespeare, A Midsummer Night's Dream

BOTTOM, THOU ART TRANSLATED

Writers are always asked how they became writers. They're asked to isolate a specific moment or set of circumstances in their biography that may have been responsible for their decision to devote themselves to writing. Translators are rarely or never asked that question, but that doesn't mean they don't ask it of themselves.

As a child I read a lot of translated books, unaware that they were translations. The communist authorities in my native country were too busy censoring books for adults to worry about *Winnie the Pooh* or *Pippi Longstocking* corrupting young minds, so a lot of classics of children's literature were published. My first conscious encounter with translation took place in a high school Russian class. Like all Polish students, I had no choice but to begin studying Russian in the fifth grade.

The decision to introduce Russian into elementary schools was politically motivated like most educational decisions in the countries of the Soviet camp. No one wanted to learn Russian, but my high school teacher, a freshly minted graduate of Jagiellonian University, made us read and memorize Russian poetry. Rather than the politically correct poets in our textbook, she preferred the politically incorrect Pushkin, and occasionally slipped in a poem by Mandelstam and Akhmatova. I loved her class, and I remember learning by heart the letter that Tatyana wrote Eugene Onegin. I later checked the Polish translation of *Onegin*, I believe by the poet Adam Ważyk, from my school library and compared it with the original. This was my very first attempt at translation criticism, if you will. After two years teaching high school, my unorthodox Russian teacher decided not to return from an organized tour to Vienna, and we were left in the hands of a woman, an orthodox party member, who made us hate her classes. By then I had also decided, together with many of my classmates, that learning the language of our oppressors was unpatriotic. I wish I had followed instead the advice of my history teacher who, fluent in Russian, would always tell us that we should know the language of the enemy.

Many years later as a college student majoring in English, I became a regular reader of the monthly *Literatura na Swiecie* (*World Literature*) which published only translations. Whenever I could get hold of the original, I'd sit down and examine the two texts side by side. I recall doing this to an excerpt from J. P. Donleavy's *The Ginger Man* and an early Ian McEwan story. I scrutinized them out of curiosity, not because I envisioned becoming a translator myself. At that time I knew nothing about the process of translation. I thought that translating meant substituting the words of one language for those of another. So each time I "caught" the translator using a word that departed from the original word's dictionary meaning, I congratulated myself. I behaved like many reviewers of translated books: they focus on individual words, and finding discrepancies between the dictionary definitions and the words used by a translator, they deem the translation poor. When I began working on my own translations, I very quickly learned that whatever is written in the source language can't be transplanted through lexical equivalents.

Looking back, I realize I might have never become a translator if I hadn't come to the United States. Any immigrant will attest that her life is a life *of* and *in* translation. The original Latin meaning of *translatus* as "carried across" fittingly depicts the situation of those who find themselves in a foreign environment. Immigrants engage in translation on a daily basis, translating the alien culture into a set of intelligible references. They also have to translate their old selves into a foreign idiom if they don't want to be like Shakespeare's Bottom, who, outwardly "translated" by Puck, remains unfazed by his new circumstances in Titania's fairy kingdom and steadfastly clings to his former identity. Immigrants' lives are exercises in the art of compromise between the pull of the new and that of the old. They are receptive and open to the new environment, and yet unable and unwilling to let go of the place they come from. Seeing double, feeling double, an awareness of loss and gain, what could be a better metaphor for translation?

This doubling—this straddling of two different worlds— more than anything else has sparked my interest in translation. Translation has accomplished two things for me: it has re-connected me with my native language and has allowed me to create a home for myself in English. But without one book, my decision to translate might have come much later than it did.

A friend gave me *Zagłada*, a novel by the Polish writer Piotr Szewc. I loved it so much that on the spur of the moment I decided to translate it. It's a small book, a little over a hundred pages, very dense, bordering on poetic prose, and it took me close to nine months to finish it. I remember how much time I spent on the title before I finally came up with *Annihilation*. The Polish word "zagłada" implies complete destruction, but if spelled with the capital Z, it also means the Holocaust, and both these meanings have to be taken into account. The Italian translator titled the book *La distruzione*, while the French translator decided to depart from the original title and settled on *L'Evanescence des choses*. Each of these choices accounts for only one segment of the title's and the book's meaning, and I have to say that my choice was more apt. The novel describes in minute detail a day in the life of a town in Poland, showing how from moment to moment nothing remains the same. It is set in the time before the Second World War, and throughout it some characters, like the Jewish owner of a fabric store, Mr. Hershe Baum, have strange dreams and premonitions about the future.

When the book was finished, I sent it to Dalkey Archive Press, and within a few weeks received a letter from John O'Brien, the publisher, telling me he wanted to publish it. After the book came out it was one of the finalists for the PEN West Translation Prize. I always thought, though, that this first translation was more a case of luck than brains, as the Polish saying goes. I groped in the dark; I knew little about the dos and don'ts of translation; I let intuition lead me. Would I change things in the book now? I'm sure I would if I were to translate it again. Translating *Annihilation*, my baptism by fire, elucidated for me the basic tenets of literary translation. I learned that literal translation doesn't create a readable text and that surface fidelity has to be sacrificed to a more profound faithfulness—to preserving the work's integrity.

At about the same time, at the urging of Szewc, who is also a poet, I began translating Polish poetry. I quickly discovered what an impossible endeavor it is. It is as if trying to reconstruct a medieval cathedral, we had only wood as our building material. No two languages are alike, but Polish and English share fewer similarities than, let's say, Polish and Slovak. If we just look at syntax, we'll see that because Polish is heavily inflectional, its word order can be manipulated (In English "John beats Jack" means something very different from "Jack beats John"; in Polish "Janek bije Jacka" and "Jacka bije Janek" have the same meaning—the word endings indicate who is on the receiving end of the action). Polish writers then can manipulate the word order at will. The translator, though, has no choice but to follow the fairly inflexible order of an English sentence. Other grammatical considerations such as number, case, and gender come into play as well. All nouns in Polish are saddled with gender, and in most cases that has little impact on translation. But sometimes gender becomes important. As in many other languages, "death" in Polish is feminine, so the Grim Reaper is a woman. You can imagine what mental acrobatics a translator has to perform when dealing with the Polish death, notwithstanding her most likely more delicate, womanly touch. And what about the mood, the voice, the tone? What about words whose meanings and connotations never overlap? When we consider all these variables, it's easy to conclude that only reckless and foolhardy people decide to be translators.

A popular opinion holds that only poets should translate other poets, and maybe in an ideal world that would be the case. Polish, unfortunately, doesn't belong to the group of world languages that are studied by many people like, for instance, French or German. By virtue of their popularity these languages lure more poet-translators, while the majority of translators of Polish poetry aren't poets. Yet these translators, such as Clare Cavanagh or Bill Johnson, have produced superb renditions of Polish poems that are on a par with any translations done by poets. Translators have to have the nature of a chameleon; they have to change depending on whom and what they translate. They have to have the ability to speak in different voices and adopt different personas. Many poet-translators have that gift and felicitously convey the original poet's voice. Yet some can only translate another poet into themselves. The translated poem may sound great, but it sounds just like the poet who translated it, not like the poet who wrote it. I'll refrain from quoting any names, but both poets and translators could come up with quite a few. Every so often a poet who doesn't know the language will collaborate with a non-poet who is fluent in the source language. There have been many such tandems that produced magnificent translations of poetry, for example, Max Hayward and Stanley Kunitz, who translated Akhmatova.

I'm often asked why I translate primarily into English and not into Polish since the latter would seem natural for someone whose native language is Polish. I answer by saying that English-language literature has a plethora of translators into Polish; it's enough to walk into any bookstore in Poland. Books translated from Polish, on the other hand, rarely grace the shelves of American bookstores. Last spring I participated in an online interview in which many different translators were asked if they considered themselves bilingual. I answered that I didn't because my Polish is much more visceral or intuitive than my English.

A quote from Vladimir Nabokov's *Lectures on Russian Literature* sums up my feelings perfectly. Nabokov, a great writer and stylist in English, even though it wasn't his native language, says: "The English at my disposal is certainly thinner than my Russian: the difference being, in fact, that which exists between a semi-detached villa and a hereditary estate, between self-conscious comfort and habitual luxury." In some sense then I may be considered an impostor since I translate into the language I wasn't born into. But does that differ from writing in the language that isn't our own? Besides Joseph

Conrad, numerous other writers did just that. Samuel Beckett wrote his plays in French; Milan Kundera now writes his novels in French, having abandoned his native Czech; Yiyun Li came to America from China at the age of twenty-four and has since become a successful writer in English, her adopted language. Poets rarely change languages, yet after living in the United States for some time, Joseph Brodsky wrote some poems in English.

So the question is, can a non-native speaker be a successful translator into the language which isn't her mother tongue? There are many examples of those who are. The majority of them consult a native speaker, another writer or poet, as I always do, although there have been those, who, like Nabokov, translated unaided by anyone. I have never read Nabokov's translation of *Eugene Onegin*, but here's what Edmund Wilson had to say about it in *The New Yorker*:

> [Nabokov's translation], though in certain ways valuable, is something of a disappointment; and the reviewer, though a personal friend of Mr. Nabokov . . . and an admirer of much of his work, does not propose to mask his. Mr. Nabokov decided that this could not be done with any real fidelity to the meaning and undertook to make a "literal" translation which maintains an iambic base but quite often simply jolts into prose. The results of this have been . . . disastrous. It has produced a bald and awkward language which has nothing in common with Pushkin or with the usual writing of Nabokov. One knows Mr. Nabokov's virtuosity in juggling with the English language, the prettiness and wit of his verbal inventions.

If we're to take Edmund Wilson's word for it, Nabokov might have been better off if he had conferred with an American poet. Supposedly the best translation of Pushkin's poem is the one done by Walter W. Arndt, whom Nabokov criticized for giving up the literalness in favor of melody and rhyme.

The Polish poet Czesław Miłosz, the 1980 winner of the Nobel Prize for Literature, was obviously not a native speaker of English, yet he was an accomplished translator of Polish poetry. He never tried writing his own poems in English, but he translated many Polish poets and also translated himself. Unlike Nabokov, he always collaborated with American poets such as Leonard Nathan, Robert Pinsky, and Robert Hass. When I visited him in 1997 in Berkeley, I asked him about this collaboration. He said he first translated the poems on his own and then asked for input from his American colleague.

Those who know little about translation are often surprised that different translators produce different versions of the original text. I once heard someone say that even if they were to translate the instructions on how to glue a stamp onto an envelope, no two translators would come up with the same version.

*

Many years ago Princeton University Press published Horace's *Odes*. There shouldn't be anything surprising about this—after all, the *Odes* have been regularly re-issued and re-translated. This time, however, the book's editor, J. D. McClatchy, asked thirty-five well-known American poets to translate the *Odes*. One may wonder which of them is closest to Horace's own, but the more important fact is that they give us a Horace we can fall in love with. When I was reading that book, I remembered a comparison that a French writer whose name I don't recall had made. He compared translators to pirates eagerly waiting to capture a ship and replace its original crew with their own. Each translator will have a different crew, and the biggest issue is whether this crew will manage to take the ship to its new destination.

Over the years I've managed to replace the crews of several books and poems, and to continue with that metaphor I had to deal with the original boats' captains. Some of them have been easy to work with, understanding the importance of the boat's arrival at a foreign shore; some others put up a fight. Working with Janusz Szuber, whose book *They Carry a Promise* was published by Knopf in 2009, has always been smooth. I could call him at any time, and he would always sound as if my phone call were the one he'd been waiting for. He answered all my interpretive questions with great clarity and precision. He doesn't know English, so sometimes I talked to him about my textual decisions. We had a good working relationship, and I can only say I wish some other writers were like Janusz. I once worked on a prose piece with a writer who was a real pain in the neck. He knew English and questioned all my choices to the extent that I finally told him he should translate himself. Another poet, whom I translated, answered my questions with a lengthy exegesis of the poem in question. This poet also knew English, but not enough to understand what I was doing. I concluded that sometimes it might be better for translators if the writers they translate know no English since if they do, they sometimes assume that their English is good enough to interfere in the translation.

Joseph Brodsky was apparently quite difficult to work with. Daniel Weissbort, his translator, says in *Translating Poetry*, the book he edited: ". . . Brodsky found it hard, or impossible, to accept his translator's notion of what was tolerable in English. He was constantly, it seemed to me, trying as it were to trans-form English into Russian, to colonize English and oblige it to do things I did not believe it could do."

Another writer notorious for his bad relationship with translators is Milan Kundera. For Kundera, translators are a suspect breed, a necessary evil, and he would frequently lash out at them in his essays. He got so paranoid that he kept changing translators for each of his books. So being aware of potential trouble, I appreciated working with Janusz Szuber.

Having said that, I have to admit that although I called him very often and sometimes consulted him about minute matters, I still managed to make some interpretive mistakes. In his poem "I Began?" he mentions *popielica*, which in Polish can mean either a plant or a gray squirrel, a dormouse. The plant fit the context perfectly, to my way of thinking, so I didn't bother to ask the author. I went even further: to preserve an alliteration that would mimic the one in the original poem, I changed the plant to one that had an "f" in it. The poem was published in *Image*. Some time later I happened to mention it to Janusz and to my dismay discovered that he had the animal in mind. I explained my reasoning to him, and Janusz decided that for the Knopf collection we should keep the plant in the poem.

Poetry loves ambiguity, and that obviously adds to the difficulty. The ambiguity may be local, attached to a word or phrase, or it may operate on the level of the whole poem. By pinning a certain interpretation onto a poetic line, the translator runs the risk of depriving the poem of its ambiguity. Being able to communicate with the poet helps solve the problem to some extent; the translator can at least know "what the poet had in mind." But certain ambiguities should still remain. The Italian writer and translator Claudio Magris said in an interview that "a text's ambiguity . . . must be respected without explaining and without simplifying, because obscurity must somehow remain."

Another translator, Miller Williams, believed in the principle of compensation. If a certain ambiguity couldn't be preserved in the exact same spot it appeared in the original, he suggested finding a place in the poem where an English word with double meaning could be used. This principle can also operate on other levels of the poem—its sound, for example. If the poet uses alliteration and the translator cannot replicate it in the same place in the poem, he or she may use alliteration elsewhere and thereby make up for what was lost. If that seems like too radical a notion, let me quote Umberto Eco, himself a translator, who says in *Experiences in Translation*, ". . . the translator must not waste too much time trying to avoid gaining something, because when translating, one is not so much likely to gain as to lose something."

*

If translation were just a bridge between two languages, the translator's task would be much easier. But this bridge spans much more than two different languages; it connects two cultures, two different ways of seeing the world, two different sensibilities. If we understand culture broadly as involving social conventions, literature, history, aesthetics, anthropology, and even etymology, then transplanting one culture into another requires that the translator be able to recognize all contextual and cultural references in the text he or she wants to translate. Does that mean that a translator equipped with this kind of knowledge can fully recreate the original text and make it fully understandable within the framework of another culture? The harsh truth translators learn to live with is that no translation can ever transfer the cultural uniqueness and reproduce the totality of a foreign text, and that absolutist demands are naive and unrealistic.

Those of us who have ever attempted translating jokes know that in most cases they are untranslatable. Sometimes the linguistic layer can't be transferred into another language, but more often than not it's the cultural context that gets in the way of understanding and creates the greatest hurdle. And political jokes tend to be even more difficult to follow unless the listener knows the larger context the jokes allude to.

The Polish poet and writer Antoni Słonimski, considered the wittiest man in pre-war Poland, spent the war years abroad, first in France and, after France's surrender, in England. In 1951 at the height of sovietization he suddenly returned to Poland. His friends in Warsaw thought he must have lost his mind. When they asked him why he'd made this foolish decision, he replied: over there no one laughed at my jokes. He preferred to live in a country where he knew his words would be censored than where his sense of humor would go unappreciated. Many years later, as punishment for his vocal opposition to the communist system, his name disappeared from school textbooks and he wasn't allowed to publish. He would often joke that the only book in which his name still appeared was the telephone directory. His name joined the list of many other writers' names, both in Poland and abroad, which the communists wanted to sentence to oblivion. All Polish émigré writers, just by virtue of living abroad, belonged to this group. The only exception to this rule was if the writer in question was to be criticized. Other writers in Poland were in a slightly better situation because they at least could publish. Their work, however, had to undergo a censor's scrutiny.

Censorship came to Poland with the Red Army and by 1945 it was firmly entrenched. It affected all areas of life and became so pervasive that until 1975 even instructions for operating electrical devices and food labels were censored. Can you imagine the paranoia of the political system which assumes that the label on a jar of mayonnaise or instructions for operating a washing machine can be seditious? When we think of censorship we tend to equate it with suppressing information, banning certain books and articles or excising the unorthodox passages. But censorship within the Soviet bloc went much farther. It was also prescriptive and preventive. It instructed writers what subjects could be written about and how they were to be approached and treated. All religious topics and the Catholic Church were out of bounds. The Soviet concentration camps had to be labeled "internment camps." If Katyń, the place of a mass execution of Polish officers by the NKVD in 1940, was ever to be mentioned, the Nazis were to be presented as the crime's perpetrators. In 1968 when student protesters at Warsaw University were brutally attacked by the police, the newspapers mentioned instances of vandalism. Some subjects could never be discussed in major publishing venues, but were allowed in specialized, low circulation journals or in local publications. Statistics were changed, history was re-written, no criticism of the Soviet Union ever saw print. The image of Poland, along with the other countries of the Soviet bloc, had to be uniformly positive, even though people were miserable and everyone was familiar with the shortages of basic goods and long lines. Censorship operated in great secrecy, and the average person wasn't supposed to know that everything—radio, TV, movies, theater, the news—was censored. Intellectuals, writers, and artists opposed censorship, but could do very little. In the seventies and eighties their answer to censorship was the development of underground publishing, the so-called second network, the samizdat, which grew to an unprecedented size.

One might think that censorship would silence writers, and that no great literary works would be created during this oppressive time. Fortunately, nothing like that happened. Writers looked at censorship as a challenge that demanded from them indirectness and obliqueness. To be published, they had to outsmart the censors and "tell all the truth but tell it slant," following the advice of Emily Dickinson, given—obviously—for very different reasons. I'm the last person to praise censorship, but it was responsible for the style of writing that became the signature style of Eastern Europe, where writers had to resort to allusion, irony, metaphor. The assumption was that "we" would get the irony and pick up on the allusions whereas "they" wouldn't. Leszek Kołakowski, the Polish philosopher, who for many years taught at Oxford, wrote an essay, "The Priest and the Jester," in which he juxtaposes the jester who is a skeptic, a Hamlet-like figure questioning everything, and the priest—a believer, an ideologue. This metaphor can also be interpreted as brilliantly capturing the situation of the artist and the censor. The writer had to resort to all sorts of "tricks" to evade the censor, and he addressed his work to those who knew how to read between the lines. Back then people in Poland were so used to looking for irony and allusion that they often found it where none was intended and where there were no hidden references to the Polish political situation.

Ryszard Kapuścinski makes a reference to this "obsession with allusion" in his book *Travels with Herodotus*. He mentions that the translation of Herodotus' *Histories* was submitted to the Czytelnik publishing house in 1951, but it didn't appear in print until after Stalin's death in 1953. According to Kapuścinski, the censors knew all too well how this book about tyrants and dictators would be read by Polish readers. In the September 24, 2007, issue of the *New Republic*, I happened across a review of *Travels with Herodotus*, which had been published earlier that year by Knopf. The reviewer, G. W. Bowersock, says something that has a direct bearing on what I've been talking about:

> I must say that reading the text of Herodotus as a text "utterly different from what was clearly written" takes a colossal effort on the part of someone reared outside a totalitarian regime . . . If there was one thing he was not, it was allusive for the purpose of conveying hidden meanings.

Bowersock is a historian so he wants to view historical facts as rooted in their time and place. Kapuścinoki, however, sees distant historical events clothed in modern garb. The author and the reviewer obviously don't share the same cultural assumptions about the meaning and lessons of history.

In his book *The Theater of Essence*, Jan Kott, the Polish theater critic and essayist who left Poland in 1966 and for many years taught at SUNY Stonybrook, comments on a performance of *Hamlet* that was staged in Kraków at the end of September 1956. In February of the same year Kruschev attacked Stalin during the Twentieth Congress of the Soviet Communist Party, and what later came to be known as the "thaw" began:

> When the line "Something is rotten is the state of Denmark" was uttered onstage, a murmur rippled through the audience from the gallery . . . When, later, the line "Denmark's a prison" was repeated three times, I felt the house go silent, like the sudden lull before a storm . . . In another moment the entire auditorium had broken into a fierce applause that lasted until hands went numb.

Obviously for this audience Shakespeare's world was real and near; it was the world they could identify with and re-interpret to suit their own situation.

So what can a translator do when dealing with a text ripe with double meanings when even a stage adaptation can be re-interpreted and re-translated by its viewers? The translator of prose is in a more comfortable position than the translator of poetry because he can provide more or less extensive footnotes or notes that explain certain political contexts and allusions. Poetry translators as a rule try to avoid notes. But even with notes the experience of an English-speaking reader won't replicate the native reader's experience, and the translator has to accept that.

Let me complicate matters even further by quoting two other examples. In his poem "Transformations of Livy" Zbigniew Herbert talks about different readings of the same historical text. Here the readers belong to the same culture—they're all Polish—but a generational divide separates his great grandfather and grandfather from his father and himself in their interpretations of Livy's *History of Rome*. He and his father "read Livy against Livy": they sided with and were moved by those whom the Romans defeated, not by Roman victories. Some familiarity with Poland's history can aid a foreign reader in understanding the poem, but even without this knowledge, the poem will speak to such a reader. The reader will be able to understand that people from nations which were treated badly by History will interpret Livy according to their own historical experience.

Another Herbert poem, "Report from a Besieged City," translated by John and Bogdana Carpenter, has the following lines:

> our
> friends beyond the sea I know they sincerely sympathize
> they send us flour lard sacks of comfort and good advice
> they don't even know their fathers betrayed us
> our former allies at the time of the second Apocalypse
> their sons are blameless they deserve our gratitude
>   therefore we are grateful

Will many foreign readers understand that the betrayal Herbert mentions is an allusion to the Yalta and Potsdam agreements? Most likely not. But the ones who do grasp the allusion will know that Churchill and Roosevelt's acceptance of Stalin's idea about the future division of Europe into two zones of influence was concomitant with assigning Poland to the Soviet zone of occupation and control. Familiarity with this fact can enhance the experience of reading the poem, but knowing it isn't indispensable to the appreciation of its greatness. John and Bogdana Carpenter understood that and refrained from attaching any notes to it.

Here we had two examples of possible under-interpretation by a foreign reader. Sometimes a reverse process may take place. If the foreign audience or the readers have the necessary background, they may over-interpret a text. That happened to a poem by Adriana Szymańska titled "Regulations" that I translated many years ago and published in *TriQuarterly*. The poet told me she had never thought of this poem in terms of a possible political context, but American readers who were familiar with Poland's political situation interpreted the poem as strictly political and equated the speaker's death wish with the desire to escape an oppressive totalitarian country:

Through the window of my cell
the precipice of eight stories aims at me
It's deadly
Maybe even more than this cosmic bluff
At midnight
the dutiful universe through a rooster's cry announces
the unchangeable order
Down there a sentry marches according to the
    regulations
back and forth on the frontline
Regulation sleep bores through the hearts of regulation
    victims
Only someone's criminal longing for freedom
whirling above the sleeping heads
rattles the walls
I could bring myself to that and
breaking the window let my body flicker like a star

in the weary eyes of the soldier
But I'm prohibited by the regulations of love
knotting right next to me the breaths of a man and a
    child
tying piles of indispensable activities
to my knees my feet my hands
an indispensable fear
to my thoughts

*

Faced with the onerous task of making one culture communicate with another, how does one go about translating cultural
references? There are two schools of thought here. One claims
that the translator should find the cultural equivalents in the
other culture and thus domesticate the references. The other
believes in preserving "the otherness" of the original text,
and—instead of leveling differences—offering the reader the
experience of the foreign. Consequently, the translator then
looks for the cultural equivalents of only those references that
otherwise would make the text unintelligible. W. S. Merwin's
translation of Osip Mandelstam's poem "Insomnia and Homer"
provides a good example for the former. Mandelstam says "na
golowach cariej bozhestviennaja piena," which literally means
"on the tsars' heads divine foam." Merwin translates "tsars" as
"leaders" in an attempt to broaden the context. The line then
reads as "leaders drenched in the foam of the gods." Another
translator rendered the same line using "kings" instead of
tsars: "Your kings' heads wreathed in spray" which is also the
choice that Mandelstam's Polish translator made ("I spływa
piana bogów po królewskiej głowie").
    I don't feel total allegiance to either one of these theories. I
know that theory and practice are often strange bedfellows. If
I had to explain my theoretical leanings, I'd say mine fall in the

middle. I want the translated text to be understood without explanatory footnotes—footnotes in poetry should be the translator's last resort—yet I also believe in preserving something of the text's "otherness" or "foreignness" to let its readers feel that they are in the presence of a culture that isn't theirs.

Translators of children's books always replace foreign cultural references with the ones children can understand and relate to. Polish children in the fifties or sixties wouldn't have any experience with a breakfast cereal eaten with cold milk, but they would know "kaszka manna" or "cream of wheat"; they wouldn't know a hot dog so "parówka" or "serdelek," a wiener or a frankfurter, would have to do. When I was working on the translation of Janusz Szuber's poem "On Vena, a Doberman Bitch," I had to find an equivalent for the Polish word "półgęsek." Półgęsek is half of a duck, deboned, smoked, with skin intact. These days not many people in Poland have tasted this delicacy, but they still recognize the word. I came up with "plump capons" which today has about the same currency in English as "półgęsek" has in Polish, and few Americans have actually eaten capons.

To continue with culinary matters, here's an example from the book *Ocalone w tłumaczeniu* by Stanisław Barańczak, the Polish poet and translator. Barańczak gives an example that shows how linguistic, textual, and cultural considerations affect a translator's choice. He discusses Wislawa Szymborska's poem "Surplus" in which she uses "orzeszki ziemne" or peanuts in English. The literal meaning of "orzeszki ziemne" is "earthnuts" and the poet uses that word for a reason. Although the word "earthnuts" can be found in an English dictionary, it's not in common use. But in the context of the poem, the "earth" component becomes indispensable, and "peanuts" just won't do. Barańczak and his co-translator, Clare Cavanagh, found a brilliant solution to this challenge:

> mostly chat on earthbound topics
> surrounded by cozy earthtones

Let me use still sanother example that shows the importance of knowing the culture one translates. It comes from Burton Raffel's book *The Art of Translating Prose*. Raffel uses the name of an institution that deprives many of sleep—the Internal Revenue Service. If a translator doesn't know the cultural context of the phrase, he or she could possibly assume that judging by the meanings of the individual words here, the phrase refers to "some helpful government activity having to do with purely domestic . . . income." A similar example from Polish could be "Urząd Stanu Cywilnego," which in Poland encompasses Register of Deeds or Hall of Records, as it may be called in different parts of the United States, as well as a place where people get married. To someone unfamiliar with the cultural context, these words could possibly mean an office where citizens may go to discuss their civic concerns.

The translator must also be able to recognize clichés. A clichéd expression in one language may have an astounding freshness in another. My husband, the novelist Steve Yarbrough, loves the Polish cliché "To stare like a calf at a painted gate" which means to stare at something awed and dumbstruck. But whenever possible a clichéd phrase should be translated into a cliché in the target language. Joseph Conrad quite frequently used Polish clichés in his writing, but in English they sounded interesting and original. In *The Nigger of the Narcissus* he has one character, James Waite, say to another: "I didn't tend pigs with you" ("Nie pasłem z tobą świn), which has no real equivalent cliché in English. In Polish the phrase is used if someone wants to assert his superior position, suggesting that familiarity is out of place as the two people aren't on the same social footing. Issac Bashevis Singer, who lived on Krochmalna Street in the Jewish quarter in Warsaw until he left Poland in

1935 and immigrated to the United States, is another writer in whose work we may find many expressions that in Polish or Yiddish don't sound original at all, but become original in an English translation from Yiddish.

Translating cultural references often involves translating dialect. This is always tricky because dialects don't have equivalent dialects in another country. It would make no sense to translate the dialect of Polish mountain dwellers into the dialect of the Appalachian region or the American South. So sometimes translators use slang, with no regional connotations. Miller Williams said something very interesting on the subject. He translated Giuseppe Gioacchino Belli, a nineteenth-century poet who wrote in Romanesco. Williams maintained that the readers must still hear the dialect as those for whom it was written heard it—not as a dialect, not a minority language. Therefore, in his translation of Belli he used standard English.

What should a translator do with intertextual references, those allusions that speak to native speakers but mean little or nothing to foreigners. Again, there are different ways of approaching the problem if we don't want to rely on footnotes: to eliminate the allusions; to replace them with the lines from a text that is familiar to the readers; to translate them and not worry that they will be lost on most foreign readers. French translators, for example, will sometimes replace quotations from Shakespeare's plays with those of Racine's since every child in France has to read Racine. I read somewhere that in his plays Chekhov often used incorrect quotations from Shakespeare, not because he didn't know his Shakespeare but because his characters didn't. Yet some overzealous translators felt bound to correct those misquotations when translating Chekhov into English.

Umberto Eco in *Experiences in Translation* talks about the difficulties his translators faced when working on *Foucault's*

Pendulum. In the novel the characters use numerous literary allusions. When on a drive among the hills, they see boundless horizons "*al di là della siepe*," which literally translated means "beyond the hedge." Since this hedge hasn't been mentioned before, Eco says, the foreign readers would be completely lost. Italian readers "know that hedge very well" since it appears in the well known Giacomo Leopardi sonnet "L'Infinito." Eco goes on to say that he told his translators "that neither the hedge nor the allusion to Leopardi was important but ... insisted that the literary clue be kept." Eco's English translator, William Weaver, used a reference to Keats' poem "On First Looking into a Chapman's Homer" and translated those lines as: ". . . we glimpse endless vistas. Like Darien, Diotallevi remarked."

Quite often, in order to make the cultural reference understandable, translators choose to resort to over-translation or even a paraphrase. Let's say the Polish translator of an American novel encounters "Piggly Wiggly" with no clarifying context to help the reader figure out what kind of store it is. The translator might then over-translate by saying "a Piggly Wiggly supermarket" or "a Piggly Wiggly grocery store." I did exactly that when in Szuber's poem "Childhood Refrains," he says that his mother took English lessons under the occupation. Again, to a Polish reader it would be obvious that Szuber has the Nazi occupation in mind, but since the context might not be immediately clear to an American reader, I inserted the word "Nazi" into the line. In another Szuber poem, "The Day is Still Beautiful," he gives the brand name of a motor-cycle—a Panonia that was produced in Hungary until 1975 and was popular in Poland after the Second World War. It's a nice specific detail, but is it worth a footnote in the transla-tion? Definitely not. Another translator might try to find an American equivalent—a brand name of a motorcycle popular in America at about the same time—but for me that would carry the Americanization of the poem too far. So I decided to under-translate and use a generic motorcycle in the line that reads: "We are on a motorcycle chugging uphill."

Translation, invariably, is fed by compromise. It's a balancing act between loss and gain, with the translator hoping that her decisions will help re-create the emotional impact and the aesthetic experience of those who have read the work in the original. And since few people can heed the great Goethe's advice that "Wer den Dichter will verstehen muss ins Dichter Lande gehen" ("he who wants to understand a poet has to go to a poet's homeland"), it's the translator who brings the writer's world, in all its otherness and strangeness, to a non-native reader and takes us out of our national confines, broadening our perspective, releasing us from cultural isolation, and, in the words of Willis Barnstone, the renowned American translator, repairing our separation.

WHAT'S IN A NAME?

I suspect I got my first name for quite trivial reasons. Ewa wasn't the name of some worthy female ancestor whom my parents wanted to honor and whose example I might follow later in life. Certain first names kept recurring in the annals of my family history, but there had never been an Ewa before me.

Since naming is the symbolic granting of personhood and the lifting from anonymity, the baby's name is usually chosen well before the birth so that he or she immediately becomes a somebody and is set on a path leading towards self-recognition and self-awareness. The process of finding the right name used to be governed by a religious tradition, and in Poland a newborn was supposed to have the name of a patron saint. Each saint had a day assigned in the calendar which would become the child's name day since name days rather than birthdays were celebrated. When my parents were naming me, the rules were less rigid, and they didn't feel they had to heed them. Their own preferences determined the choice, and I don't believe they worried whether their child would be happy with her given name. They chose Ewa because they simply liked it, not because they had any interest in its biblical provenance or its Hebrew meaning. They may have also wanted to break with the tradition on Mother's side of the family where long polysyllabic girls' names were the norm. My maternal grandmother's name was Antonina, my mother's Justyna, her sister's Jadwiga. Grandmother Antonina's sisters all had long names too—Genowefa, Apolonia, and Marianna. Ewa had the desired brevity, and the added bonus was its popularity, something that may have appealed to two young people naming their firstborn. How do I know Ewa was popular? I noticed a disproportionately large number of my namesakes everywhere girls my age gathered. When I started college, out of the fourteen female students admitted to the English department at the University of Wrocław, there were five Ewa's, including me. That fact never bothered me since I knew there wasn't another Ewa like me, and I was the only Ewa Lipnicka, my identity pinned and safely circumscribed by my last name.

Many years later my parents told me that when I first learned to speak, for quite some time I didn't use *I*, but referred to myself as *Ewa*. I would say, "Ewa hungry; Ewa wants her teddy; Ewa dancing." I was too young to have even the first inkling of self-consciousness, but my mother and father interpreted my early attempts at speech as the sign of fondness for the name they had given me. Neither had any background in children's cognitive development to know that I did what children that age do. We're our first name before we arrive at the *I*.

I have always liked my name and treated it as the inseparable part of myself. My name wasn't made fun of or distorted by other children, so I never asked to be called by another. I remember only one time when I wished I had a different one. At the age of nine, I went to visit my aunt who lived in the neighboring city. On the playground in front of the apartment building where my aunt lived, I met Wioletta. All the other girls there had common names like Basia, Krysia, Ania, so hers stuck out. I thought it was the most beautiful name imaginable, and I repeated it to myself separating the syllables as if I were tasting the most delicious cream puff. The dresses she wore added to her attractiveness and made her seem even more unlike the rest of us. They all looked like Sunday best. They didn't belong on a playground where the kids mostly wore hand-me-downs, shabby pants and tops, or scruffy warm-ups. Wioletta's mother, it turned out, was a seamstress, and her daughter could daily parade around in dresses that her mom had sewn and that most of us could only dream of. Wioletta would have probably remained the object of my admiration and envy longer than the week's stay with my aunt if very soon after I met her she hadn't turned out to a be mean-spirited sissy who refused to join our rough and boisterous games for fear of soiling her dress. I was unable to separate her act from her name, and that cured my infatuation. I decided I no longer liked her name and wouldn't swap my own for hers.

It was a different story with the books I read. When I identified with the heroine, the impersonation wouldn't have been complete unless I took her name. I must have sensed the magical and transformative powers of naming. If I wanted to pretend to be the Little Princess, my name had to be Sara; if I dreamed of the adventures in Wonderland, I called myself Alice. With *Anne of Green Gables* I was Anne, even though she dreamed at first of a more romantic name like Cordelia. I could empathize with her yearnings, but I shared in Marilla's no-nonsense stance that Anne was a perfectly good and sensible name which I happily adopted in order to transport myself to Avonlea.

I knew early on there weren't very many famous women named like me. The biblical first mother hardly compensated for this scarcity. In religion classes the nuns told us she was the cause of Original Sin, responsible for humankind's suffering. Because I was her namesake, I felt sorry for her. Adam's wife was criticized far too harshly. What was the big deal about taking a bite out of a juicy apple and wanting to share it with your husband? God was downright unfair when he kicked Adam and Ewa out of paradise, and for what—eating an apple?

I gave little thought to my last name. There was nothing about it that was offensive or comical and could make me the butt of jokes. Lipnicka didn't refer to anything; it had no meaning like the names of some people I knew. My high school Latin teacher's name was Szczur—Rat—but because he was universally loved, no one made fun of it. His daughter, also Ewa, who was in the same grade as I, seemed not bothered by it. He did, though, change his last name when Ewa was already in college. I never wondered why it was the father's name that the mother and the children carried. I knew nothing of patriarchy and the implications of ownership that patronymics conveyed. Only unwed mothers' names were given to children, but that connoted illegitimacy.

When I married, I took my husband's last name. That's what women did back then; few names were hyphenated. I didn't give the decision much thought, and only for a very short while did I consider adding his name to mine. But Lipnicka-Hryniewicz seemed way too long. It never occurred to me to keep my family name. Even though there were so many Ewa's around, I viewed my last name as a sort of loose appendage. It's true that—if I am to wax Aristotelian—Ewa was only my *genus proximus* which needed Lipnicka, its *differentia specifica*, to make me unique, but Ewa defined me more than my surname ever did. I liked the sound of Ewa Lipnicka, but then Ewa Hryniewicz sounded good too. Getting married meant I was entering a new stage in my life, and that new stage might as well be marked by something as visible as a new last name. My circumstances were about to change, but the loss of my original family name didn't mean the loss of my identity. I would still remain Ewa, the person I was.

*

My attachment to my first name was tested when I came to the US. Until then I never suspected that it could cause anybody difficulty. The main culprit was the "w." Each time I was in a doctor's waiting room and saw a nurse's stricken-looking face, I knew she was about to try to say my name, which invariably was "youwa" or "eewa." Friends knew that the "w" was just a "v" and that the "e" should be pronounced like the one in "Emma." Some Polish Ewa's who immigrated to English-speaking countries changed the spelling of their name to Eva, but I didn't see myself as Eva. Modifying my given name would have felt like self-betrayal. Besides, the anglicized spelling did nothing to solve the problem. The long "ee" in Eva wasn't the short "e" in Ewa, and it still sounded wrong. My name was as much part of who I was as my accent. I liked it that they immediately identified me before other people as a foreigner. I never wanted to hide my foreignness under an American-sounding name. I wanted to embrace the new reality, but not at the cost of becoming someone I was not. I had no desire to shed the outward manifestations of my identity, the more so that I was aware of the many changes still in store for me because I no longer lived in the country of my birth. Even though I was already retranslating myself into another language and culture, I refused to become completely colonized. I hoped that the end product, like all good translations, would retain some of my otherness. And alongside my accent, my first name with its Polish spelling was the visible, if only token, sign of my resistance.

The earlier generations of immigrants, desperate to blend in once they arrived here, often changed their names to Anglo-sounding ones. The Polish poet Julian Tuwim used to tell a story which illustrates the immigrant's quandary. A certain Polish man named Abel immigrated to America and decided to follow the natives' clues in his attempts to join the melting pot. His name in Polish had the initial vowel "ah," but in America people pronounced it like "ay." To conform to what he heard, he changed the spelling to "Ebel." His new name was then pronounced by everyone as "Eebel." The man was persistent, and began to write it "Ibel," which would be the correct Polish spelling for "ee." Naturally, English speakers read it as "i." Following the phonetics of the Polish language, he thought he had come up with a perfect solution and wrote his name "Ajbel." When he heard it said as "edgebel," he gave up and went back home.

For the first three years here I used my married name Hryniewicz, which most Americans found unpronounceable. Thank goodness that the US is such an informal country, and one rarely has to resort to the person's last name. Eventually, I got divorced and re-married. My new husband's name, Yarbrough, difficult to pronounce for a Polish speaker, had nothing unusual about it for the natives. Since I already had to deal with Ewa, which was consistently mutilated by almost everyone except my close friends, I now could simplify things by switching to my American husband's ordinary-sounding name. That didn't happen, though. I came to America as an exchange visitor, and I was Hryniewicz on all of my documents, diplomas, transcripts, and in my Polish passport. Since altering everything would have been too much trouble, I chose the lesser evil and became hyphenated as Hryniewicz-Yarbrough. While I was still teaching, I went by Ewa H. Yarbrough because my students were intimidated by Hryniewicz.

I lasted as Hryniewicz-Yarbrough until my naturalization when I was given a chance to start afresh and jumped at it. My American passport states that I'm Ewa Yarbrough. In Poland

and in my Polish passport I continue hyphenated. I'm also hyphenated on my published work. I started out as a literary translator, and the two-part name aptly reflected the nature of what I was engaged in. I'm not troubled by having two last names: Yarbrough here and Hryniewicz-Yarbrough in Poland. Doubleness has long been a fact of my life.

I need to mention a complication in this picture: sometimes people assume I have either misspelled my first name or written it illegibly, and they correct the "w" to the "v." That's why I was Eva on my California driver's license and on a number of credit cards. I now make sure the misspellings don't happen. Yet to this day, depending on the circumstances, I catch myself checking if I need to sign my name as Ewa Hryniewicz-Yarbrough, Eva Yarbrough, Ewa H. Yarbrough, or Ewa Yarbrough. I'm the same person under all those guises, but asking which *I* am I, and which I need to go by at a given moment inevitably leads to other interesting questions about naming, belonging, and the fluidity of identity.

THE POLITICS OF HAIR

The oldest picture of Grandmother Antonina shows her with her hair close to her head, pulled back, with no parting, and delicate pencil-thick waves going all the way to the neckline, which she most likely made with heated scissor irons. This photo has no date, but I can assume it was taken before Grandmother turned twenty-four because she bobbed her hair soon after moving to Warsaw in the early 1930s. She'd gotten married a year earlier and lived for a while with her husband's family in a small town near the capital, where women still wore their hair long, just as in the village she came from. In Warsaw, though, short hair was all the rage. On her first visit home, when she proudly displayed the new style to her family, she had to listen to her mother's lengthy harangue on the evils that accompanied such an unnatural deed. Her three sisters—even the eldest—would never have thought of doing away with their braids. Their hair went down below their buttocks and they could easily sit on it. My future grandmother no longer had the protection against germs that long hair provided and could easily fall prey to all and sundry ailments, developing anemia, experiencing debilitating headaches, even becoming infertile. Grandma proved the last accusation untrue when the following year she gave birth to my mother. But my great-grandmother had it on the authority of the Church that short hair was downright unhealthy. Only women who were sick or poor cropped their hair (the wig-makers were willing to pay a pretty penny for natural hair), and my grandmother was neither.

While city attitudes toward women cutting their tresses had by then become more liberal, in small towns and villages the daring ones were branded morally delinquent and sentenced *a priori* to eternal damnation. A popular saying—"Short hair, short on brains"—expressed prevalent attitudes. No wonder my great-grandmother was upset and begged her headstrong daughter to put on a scarf when she went out. Grandmother agreed to spare her mother public disgrace: the next photo I have of her shows her in front of the family house, her head covered with a white scarf, holding my mother, who couldn't have been more than a few months old. That was the only compromise my grandmother agreed to and she ignored her mother's pleas that she grow her hair out again.

*

When my grandmother committed what to her mother was an unthinkable act, short haircuts had already been in vogue for quite a while. It all started in the 1920s when the fashion had begun to spread like a plague, the term used by its most implacable opponents. Although at first it seemed a radical novelty, women had worn their hair short before, but the cut had never become as popular as in the 1920s. During the French Revolution women had their locks cut off in back before they were led to the guillotine. This might look like a cruel and flippant example were it not for the fact that it spurred a short-lived and morbid fad, a haircut called *à la victime*. Many fashionable women chose that style to honor the victims and had their hair shorn high up at the nape of the neck with long strands on the sides of their faces. Unlike other fashions that originated in France, that one didn't catch on anywhere else. About a century later suffragettes cut their hair shoulder length, but few other women were ready to challenge the tradition and show off cropped hairdos.

Though many stylists had laid claim to "inventing" the short haircut, the man who played the greatest role in launching it was Antoni Cierplikowski. Born in 1884 in Sieradz, Poland, the son of a shoemaker, Cierplikowski left for Paris in 1901, and there his career took off as he became Monsieur Antoine, world-famous stylist and author of the *coupe à la Jeanne d'Arc*. In 1909, the story goes, Eve Lavallière, the famous French actress, forty at the time, was offered the role of an eighteen-year old heroine in the comedy *Buridan's Ass*. She wanted to accept it, but was concerned that she would end up ridiculed because of her age. When she turned for help to Antoine, who had already made a name for himself in Paris, he decided that the way to make a woman look younger was to cut her hair. That's how the famous cut was born. Its variants came to be known under numerous monikers: the bob, the Eton crop, or most popular in Europe, *à la garconne*. After the première of the play, Paris was abuzz. Eve Lavallière looked the juvenile character, and the play was a success. At first only women from Bohemian circles followed the actress's example. But in about ten years what had once been marginal turned into a trend and short haircuts began to be seen on the streets of the French capital. Coco Chanel, Antoine's friend and neighbor, championed the new hairstyle just as she championed simplicity in women's clothes. A revolution that began in fashion and hair spread to women's attitudes, lifestyles, social and sexual norms, redefining and challenging traditional gender roles.

Literature provided succor. In 1921 a novel titled *La garçonne* by Victor Margueritte appeared in France. It became a bestseller, enjoyed multiple editions and was translated into many languages. It caused a scandal too. Its heroine, Monique, is the innocent daughter of wealthy parents who plan to marry her off to a young man who doesn't love her. Before the wedding she finds out her future husband has a lover but no intention of breaking up with her. Marriage is for him a business deal. Monique rebels, leaves her family, works as an interior designer. She cuts her hair, dresses like a man, smokes, uses drugs, takes lovers and has lesbian mistresses. When the book was published in Poland, it bore the title "Chłopczyca," which can be translated into English as Tomboy or Flapper.

*

I don't believe that Monsieur Antoine, Coco Chanel, or Victor Margueritte's novel could have had any direct influence on my grandmother's decision to crop her hair. She cut it when she saw women in Warsaw sporting short styles. For most who decided to follow the craze, short hair meant more than a fashion statement. It indicated you were independent and modern. Grandmother wasn't really independent in today's sense of the word—she was a young mother whose husband worked and supported her. Yet knowing what I know about her, I can assert that she aspired to be a modern woman and wanted to be seen as such, even though it took many years before she could truly claim the adjective for herself. But even if those considerations played some role in her decision to bob her hair, they weren't the most important. What others deemed a superficial gesture was to her a deeply symbolic act which marked a watershed in her life.

In all the stories Grandmother told me about her childhood and adolescence, one detail consistently came up: her deep dislike of village life and farming. She was one of six siblings—four sisters and two brothers—and from the start she was the most rebellious. After they reached a certain age, all country children were expected to work: first in the house, then in the yard, and eventually in the fields. From the instant she was sent to join her brother and her two older sisters to hoe sugar beets, she had hated working the soil, hated how dirt got in her eyes and under her fingernails. She'd rather do any kind of housework, scrub the floors, wash everyone's clothes, slop the hogs, or clean the pigsty. But no amount of pleading would convince her parents to let her off. She was old enough, and they needed an extra pair of hands. So she had no choice but to get up at dawn and spend most of the day hoeing weeds, making haystacks, digging potatoes. Farming was backbreaking toil, and early on she began to harbor dreams of escape. A village school afforded her something of a respite: during the school year she was sent to the fields only after she had returned from her lessons. Her father had trained to be a teacher—I don't know if he ever worked as one, or even if he completed his training—but that made him do what his illiterate neighbors thought foolish: he sent his children to school even when there was work to be done in the fields. Grandmother quickly learned to read and write and enjoyed every moment she spent studying. She attended that school for four years, and then, after a two-year break due to political turmoil—in which the First World War concluded and Poland regained its independence—she finished the final years in a bigger school four kilometers away from home. She was sixteen. There was never any talk of her continuing her education, even though one of her brothers finished agricultural school and the other one became a teacher. She was a girl, and her father, progressive as he was, wasn't progressive enough to see the need for that.

She met my grandfather when she was twenty-one, but I know nothing else about their meeting or courtship. Village girls usually married when they were much younger than Grandmother, so her parents must have worried she'd be an old maid. Not that she lacked suitors. Plenty of eligible bachelors in the village tried to woo her, but she wasn't interested because they had the manners and looks of country bumpkins. Grandfather was different, though. Born in a nearby town, he had finished gymnasium, taken some accounting courses, played the accordion. He had a warm baritone, and on top of everything was drop-dead handsome. But to my grandmother the most important thing about him was that he wasn't from the countryside. Within a year of their getting married, the couple moved to Warsaw, which for her meant a clear break with peasant life, the change she had been dreaming of.

To emphasize that break, she had her hair cut. Now when she went shopping or took her daughter for a stroll in the park, she looked like other young Warsaw mothers. Although she wanted to belong in the city, she never denied her peasant origins, pretended to be someone she wasn't or put on airs. If she was vain, her vanity was limited to trying to look like a city person, but being a snob or a social climber wasn't in her blood. I have a later photo of her taken a few years before the war in which my mother, maybe four or five years old, is sitting on a donkey, Grandmother standing next to her, holding her hand. She wears a smart dark coat and a wide-brimmed hat cocked at an angle. A bit of her hair shows and I can see it's short. My mother is wearing a beret and her hair is also short, a simple bob with bangs reaching her eyebrows. No one looking at this picture would ever think that Grandmother hadn't lived in the city all her life.

*

During the war years, having no money for a professional cut, she kept her hair short by asking a friend to trim it. Early in the war Grandfather was seized in a roundup. He managed to escape from the train carrying him to Germany for forced labor but was in hiding for some time before returning home. By then he already had a reputation as a ladies' man. He also never refused a drink. The harsh conditions of life and his irresponsible behavior turned my grandmother into the self-reliant and independent woman she had always wanted to be and had the temperament and disposition for. She provided for her two daughters, the younger of whom had been born during the war. Because of permanent food shortages and rationing, she often went to the country and smuggled provisions to Warsaw, an exceedingly risky enterprise. A single photo remains from the war period: my grandmother, her hair short and wavy, is holding her bald baby daughter.

The war ended with most of Warsaw razed to the ground. Grandmother loved her city but didn't see how she could piece her life back together among the ruins. So the family decided to seek its fortunes in Eastern Pomerania. The region's former German residents fled before the approaching Red Army, leaving behind farmhouses, villas, single-family homes, apartments. The newcomers from other war-torn regions could have their pick as to where they wanted to settle. Many of those who, due to the shifting borders, had lost their family farms in the East decided to take over the deserted red-brick houses and barns with their adjoining fields. But returning to farming was out of the question for Grandmother. Since she had to give up Warsaw, the family moved to a small town in the

Mazury region where Grandfather had found a nice second-floor apartment. At that time there were still many unoccupied villas and houses with well-preserved gardens, fruit trees, shrubs, and flowers. Grandmother, however, refused to even consider living in a house. Many of these homes were elegant and spacious. The gardens, though, were the biggest stroke against them, since a garden meant you'd have to tend it and work the soil, something Grandmother had sworn off many years ago.

In 1951 she divorced Grandfather, the final step on her way to independence. She was never very religious, but she'd been raised in church and went to Sunday mass. Few people at that time got divorced, but Grandmother had suffered enough of the ordeal her marriage had become. A year or so before she made up her mind, she went to confession, where she told the priest about her husband's unfaithfulness and drinking and added that she was thinking of divorcing him. The priest's response infuriated her when he said that bad as her marriage sounded, it was her cross to bear. That encounter was enough to turn her anti-clerical. For many years afterwards, she only attended church for baptisms, weddings, and funerals. But her divorce didn't only defy the precepts of the church; it also went against traditional ways of thinking and the social mores of the times. Even though the communists allowed civil marriage and divorce, the nascent political order exhibited extreme prudishness and puritanical orthodoxy when it came to family morals. Respectable people—and good communists—just didn't file for divorce. A divorced woman was suspect: she might go after another woman's husband, and that could be reason enough to ostracize her. Grandmother—fortunately—didn't suffer such a fate. She was generous, helpful, and well-liked by neighbors, co-workers, and whoever else crossed her path. And she must have loved her hard won autonomy and self-sufficiency so much that she never remarried.

*

When I was a few years old, Grandmother began to take me to a hair salon five minutes away from our apartment building. The shop was in a garden where its owner, Mr. Żebrowski, grew vegetables and fruit for his family. It had two rooms: a barber shop in the front where men congregated, and a room in back where women came and had their hair styled. Because Grandmother believed in no-nonsense haircuts for girls, we never entered the women's section. I was seated on a padded board placed across the arms of a chair, dangling my legs. It would be some time before I would be tall enough to occupy the leather-covered seat reserved for adults. Mr. Żebrowski, who always cut my hair, wrapped me in what looked like a white sheet and pinned it at my neck. He then looked at my grandmother occupying a bench against the wall. "How will we cut the young lady's hair today?" he asked her each time, even though he knew the answer would be "*Na garsonkę*"—*à la garconne*. My hair wasn't long, but according to her, the curls had become unruly. I didn't mind their being cut off. Some would still remain. The part I hated was when the barber used the razor on the nape of my neck. It pinched and I cringed. He then brushed my neck to get the clippings off and sprayed perfume over my head, squeezing an egg-shaped brown rubber ball attached to a half-full glass bottle. The procedure was finished when he picked me up and placed me on the floor. I was very proud of myself. I had an elegant hairdo just like Grandmother's. On the way home we always stopped at a small grocery store where I got my favorite chocolate-covered candy bar called *Krymski*—Crimean.

We repeated the same ritual about once every two months until I was old enough to go to Mr. Żebrowski's on my own. Each time I went I was handed five złoty for a haircut and five to keep. The money replaced the candy bar. Years later it occurred to me that just like the chocolate bar the five złoty was a bribe Grandmother used to make sure I wore my hair short. My short hair wasn't anything unusual. The photos I have from that time show most girls with bobs. In my preschool photo, there's only one girl with a braid. In the group picture of my first grade I can see two girls wearing plaits. The reason most likely wasn't so much the fashion of the time as the fact that many mothers and grandmothers had jobs, and there was no one at home to braid a little girl's hair to make her look neat for school. This was the time when posters of women on tractors became ubiquitous, but the propaganda of the brave new world had little to do with women's decision to find employment. Besides, only true believers could have been swayed by it. Since one income wasn't enough to support a family, most women started to work for economic reasons. Eventually, many of them decided that they liked the feeling of independence and the social interaction that came with it. What began as a necessity turned into a boon that fired many women's aspirations toward self-sufficiency and self-reliance.

My grandmother was at home a lot, but she was philo-sophically opposed to long hair and might have only reluc-tantly agreed to braid it. She wore her own hair short, not because she felt she still needed to affirm her city-ness but for its associations with independence and practicality. She also favored simply cut clothes that Coco Chanel would have liked, and she used only a lipstick and an eyebrow liner for makeup. It's not that looks didn't matter to her. She learned the ways of the world well enough to know that a certain elegance was necessary if one wanted to communicate confidence. Since her program for women was anti-narcissistic, there was no place in it for long hair which played up feminine features and was bound to lead to undue focus on one's looks. A woman could accomplish anything if she didn't think too much about herself, worked hard, and took charge. Grandmother never heard of feminism, but she rejected wholesale the stereotype of the weaker sex.

I imbibed her lessons on hair and life, but when I was in fourth grade, I decided to grow my hair out, even though all my friends had bobs. I got interested in history, and all the famous queens, princesses, and duchesses had long hair. At first I wore pigtails, which in due time metamorphosed into two braids. Because my hair was longer then, it was more tangled than ever before, and I hated it when my mother combed it each morning. I also didn't like it that I had to get up earlier so that it could be braided before school. I endured until early June. Three weeks before summer vacation I told Grandmother I needed to see Mr. Żebrowski. I didn't want to go to a Girl Scouts' camp with long hair. It would be too much trouble. Grandmother didn't show it, but as she handed me ten złoty, I could tell she was elated at my newly acquired practical sense.

I continued to wear my hair short even when the hippie fashion, as we called it, arrived in our town and teenage girls tried to imitate the hairstyles of famous American female singers like Joan Baez and Janice Joplin. Grandmother didn't approve of the fad. This was when she modified the saying "Short hair, short on brains" that had such a currency in her youth into "Long hair, short on brains." My first year in college, though, I let my hair reach beneath my shoulders. When I came home for Christmas, she shook her head. "You look like a mermaid," she said. I knew it wasn't a compliment. I cut it again before the next fall semester began, not because my grandmother didn't like it but simply because it dawned on me I had no patience for long hair. Come to think about it now, maybe Grandmother did have something to do with my decision. It couldn't have been coincidental that all the women in our family, my mother, my aunt, my sister and I had always preferred short hair. As for Grandmother's own style, it remained unchanged: *à la garconne*, with a parting on the side. She never bothered changing it, saying she was happy with what she had.

*

When she was in her mid-eighties, Grandmother developed an eczema that spread onto her scalp and was responsible for gradual hair loss. She had reddish-pinkish bald patches, with tufts of hair like a newborn's surrounding them. No medication worked. When she was hospitalized for a heart problem, which ultimately involved putting her on a pacemaker, a young attending doctor noticed the eczema and said she might be allergic to dairy products. On his orders she was put on a dairy-free diet, and within a week the patches on her head receded. The doctor then advised her to continue the regimen. After Grandmother was checked out, my aunt stayed with her for a few days and made sure she had no milk and cheese. The eczema had disappeared. When my aunt returned in two weeks, Grandmother's scalp was aflame again. She had gone back to drinking milk and eating cheese. She refused to listen to any arguments. She was too old, she said, to give up what she liked. My aunt tried to persuade her by saying that her hair would grow back only to hear that she didn't care.

Each time I visited Grandmother with my American family, she would put on a wig. She said that she didn't want our two daughters to think their great-grandmother was a bald witch. She also made everyone promise she would be buried in her wig. One summer I arrived in Poland ahead of the rest of my family and went to see her by myself. I expected to find her wearing her wig, but she had a scarf on. I had never seen her wearing scarves before since in her universe they were worn by country women. I figured it was gentler and easier on her scalp than a wig. But as long as she wore a wig, she looked like her old self because the wig mimicked her natural hair. A scarf, however, changed her appearance so much that she seemed a different person. It saddened me that she had to cover her head with a piece of fabric she wouldn't have been caught dead in before. She used to have such beautiful hair, dark blond, naturally wavy, and she always wore hats or elegant caps.

When I embraced her, I could feel her bones. She seemed birdlike, smaller and frailer than during my last visit, but maybe I just hadn't noticed it earlier. She had turned ninety-two the previous February, and until then she had been quite robust. I suddenly had the premonition that Grandmother wouldn't be around much longer. My heart sank. She had always had an uncanny ability to read my mind and mood, and this time too she sensed that I was shaken. But she wouldn't be herself if she had let that mood last. She squeezed my hand and asked me to hand her an old photo album. She leafed through it, found the page she wanted, and gave it back to me, pointing to a picture. It showed her standing in front of her family house, holding my mother and wearing a white scarf. She gestured toward her head. "I'm now back to my young days. My mother didn't like my bob, so I covered it." She gazed at the ceiling. "Mom must be having a good chuckle up there now. Her daughter is at last getting her deserts." She laughed, and so did I. She displayed her usual panache and sense of humor. I was relieved that she still could slip so easily into her customary groove.

I called her regularly all throughout the following year. When I talked to her on her birthday, she told me she would be moving in with my aunt at the end of February. I knew that for a long time my aunt had been begging her to do it, but each time Grandmother said no. She liked living by herself even though she no longer could do everything she wanted. Her decision meant she was forced to admit that she had become weaker and needed help.

My last conversation with her took place that year at the end of August. She didn't sound like herself. Her voice, always so peppy and full of life, kept fading, and she spoke with difficulty.

She died in the second week of November. She was buried in her wig, styled the way she liked—*à la garconne*.

SPACED OUT

The first time I ever traveled from the East coast to the West, the drive entranced me. We were moving from Chapel Hill, North Carolina, to Fresno in California's Central Valley. Even though we had our six-month old daughter and my eleven-year old Polish nephew in tow, on whose care we expended a lot of time and attention, I enjoyed our trip. Before we set out, my husband tried to convince me that I should take the kids and fly after he'd driven there by himself. I rejected his suggestion. I wanted to see and learn the landscape of my new country. On the way we stopped to visit my in-laws in Mississippi, but until we went farther west, the surroundings hadn't changed much along the way. It was still the southern countryside, well known to me after my combined four years in Virginia and North Carolina. Soon the distances gradually expanded and the houses grew farther apart, but the little towns we passed were all familiar looking. Each had a bank, a drugstore, a hardware, and at least one church. Once we crossed into Texas,

I expected the real West to begin, the West that I thought I knew, since as a child I'd watched a lot of westerns with my father, a movie buff, who took me to our town's theater each time a new film with John Wayne or James Stewart was shown. I was convinced I would easily recognize the landscape. But because the camera lens framed the scenery, carving out only a segment of it and in the process diminishing it, the films I saw could never show what the real place looked like.

I was therefore completely unprepared for what I encountered—the immensity of the space, the huge sky, and the unobstructed view stretching to the faraway horizon. We drove for miles without seeing a trace of human settlements—no houses to rest your eyes on, no twinkling lights of people's homes after dusk, the concrete highway the only man-made thing between distant towns. Though at first I joked about the regularly posted warnings to buy gas ahead of time, pretty quickly I understood the wisdom of heeding them. Soon we saw the mountains looming ahead, Humphrey's Peak visible for many hours before we actually came close to it. The world looked like it must have thousands of years ago: young, new, unscathed, and unscarred by human activity. Only the planes flying in the otherwise empty sky were proof of human presence. Nowhere else in America did I have this powerful impression that this indeed is the New World.

If I had hoped we'd be able to get out of the car and stop in the woods by the river, I had to give those hopes up. The terrain was bare, almost moon-like, so the only thing we could do was drive on. When driving—and we drove several hundred miles each day—you normally don't see minutia. The landscape here, though varied on a large scale, collaborated with the idea of car travel and offered almost no small details, as if in its enormity it considered them incidental and useless.

*

Since then I have traveled many times by car from California to the east and back, taking different routes, generally more northward, through Nevada, Utah, Colorado, Wyoming, Nebraska or Iowa, and each time I was awed by the vastness of the land and its raw and terrible beauty. We tend to think of space as liberating, but its inhuman dimensions overwhelmed and intimidated me. I could admire such landscape as a tourist, but I knew I wouldn't want to live in a place where the horizon is two hundred miles away. I was raised in such a thoroughly different space that I needed a landscape which seemed less threatening. In Europe it would be impossible to find such vast and uninhabited areas that extend for hundreds of miles. Even the most barren and rugged terrain there looks almost tame compared to the American wilderness which, unobstructed, keeps on opening.

*

I also see this outward opening in many American towns, those built on a grid, where the streets run along perpendicular and horizontal lines, north-south and east-west, with no center toward which everything turns, where Main Street— the axis with a bank, a post office, a drugstore, a hardware— doesn't really stop and could be built up at each end, extended according to need. European towns never had that kind of freedom. They were self-contained, self-sufficient microcosms, closed in and surrounded by walls intended to protect against the enemy but also to keep the residents within. Since the Middle Ages they have been centrally oriented toward a market square crowned by the cathedral and the town hall. Even the towns which have no medieval layout and which arose later have those types of hubs. When people settled there, they expected to remain for generations and their houses communicated permanence through their brick solidity. American towns extended different promises. Their openness connoted possibility, mobility, freedom, the birthright of the country's inhabitants. One should be able to leave at any moment, "light out for the territory," go wherever one pleased, most often in the direction of the setting sun, toward the Pacific, the vector that for years governed translocation in America to an extent that northward or southward movement didn't, at least not until the Great Migration and its aftermath. Is it any wonder then that Americans invented the mobile home and perfected the European picaresque into a road novel?

Maybe because of their openness American cities are easier to navigate, harder to get lost in. Physically and literally, I have never found myself lost in an American city, yet I often feel lost in what to me is their unfamiliar space. This feeling doesn't just arise because American cities lack architectural landmarks spanning centuries that help me orient myself in Europe or because they exhibit a certain homogeneity which to an outsider makes them look alike. The reason is that not many of them are walking cities, and for me walking is the most important factor in familiarizing myself with alien space. If the space you're in isn't designed for pedestrians, you have no choice but to drive. Driving, though, never builds the kind of connection to and knowledge of the place that comes from bodily immersing yourself in it, noticing details and absorbing them with your senses. Since exploring a place on foot has always been my way of getting to know any new area, during my first years in the United States I walked everywhere. At that time I was fortunate to live in two university towns, where pedestrians were nothing out of the ordinary. When we moved to Fresno, California, a city of about half a million people, I thought I could continue walking. But each time I set off along Blackstone Avenue, some car drivers honked as if I presented an outrageously comical sight. Only later did I find out that only hookers walked that stretch.

*

When I was growing up, I never thought we were cramped, even though my family occupied small quarters. Our two rooms and kitchen originally belonged to a larger four-room apartment, which the diligent communist authorities deemed a bourgeois frivolity and hastily partitioned to fit in two families instead of one. At first my grandmother lived there with my aunt and mother. After my mother married, my father moved in with them. The newlyweds occupied the bigger room, my grandmother the smaller one. When I was born, my crib was in my parents' room. Four years later my sister arrived, and all of us lived together until I entered fifth grade.

In college I rented a room from a young accountant. It had a built-in closet, a narrow bed, and a desk opposite the window. Two people couldn't have walked side by side along the bed. Did I dream of more space? Never. I had classmates who lived six to a dorm room and envied me my luxury. When on my first trip to the West in 1973, I was invited to an English country house for lunch, I was impressed by its size. In London, though, my English friends lived in crowded rented rooms, not much different from the ones I was used to. Many years later when I had my own apartment, which by American standards would be considered small, its modest size didn't bother me. Some people owned bigger apartments and houses, but the majority of the population lived in ridiculously confined quarters, happy that they had their own place since apartments were also on the list of shortages that plagued our lives.

The first American home I lived in was in Gainesville, Florida. I was staying for one semester with a family of a history professor there. I was amazed at the number of rooms, all assigned a specific function, not the all-purpose rooms we had in Poland. It was a two-story house with five bedrooms, a study with floor-to-ceiling bookshelves, a large living room, formal dining room, big kitchen with a breakfast nook, family room, and three bathrooms. While to its owners the space was something perfectly normal, to me it was a veritable palace. Someone might think that after returning home, I felt deprived. I didn't, even when I was describing the house to my friends or fondly reminiscing about my stay in America.

After I came to the United States, my sense of space remained rooted in my previous life. At the beginning of 1989 my American husband and I moved into our own house, a three-bedroom Tudor, with one bathroom and a small back-yard. I assumed we'd live there for many years to come, but a few years after our second daughter was born, my husband started saying the house was too small for us. I never felt cooped up in it; I thought we had plenty of room. The next house we bought seemed huge to me—three bedrooms with a large master bedroom, two bathrooms, open floor plan, big yard—though to many Californians it was just medium sized, only 2300 square feet. While I liked our new house, I often missed the intimacy of our previous home.

Today we live in an old New England house which has many small rooms with walls dividing the space and creating nooks and crannies. I feel enclosed in it as though I had been given one more protective layer, more solid than my clothes or skin. I've never felt at ease in large spaces or large gatherings of people. If at some point in my life I hoped that my relationship to space would change and that I'd develop a liking for large-ness and openness, and in the process become more outgoing myself, that hasn't happened. Culture and geography may have played some role in determining my spatial parameters, but my preferences have been shaped primarily by my personal idiosyncrasies and introverted disposition. Smallness has been and will always be my comfort zone.

I am a travel agency for the dead,
I book them flights to the dreams of the living.
—Krystyna Dąbrowska "Travel Agency"

MY PRIVATE BOOK OF THE DEAD

FATHER

Father died on April 27, five days before his name day and my birthday, both of which fell on May 2. At that time most people in Poland, unless they were Protestants, observed name days devoted to their patron saint. I did too, but because my birthday coincided with my father's name day, I celebrated both, enjoying the special distinction of being , as he put it, the best gift he'd ever received. When I went to college I couldn't return for our day. Wrocław, where I studied, was too far away. It would take about a ten hour train ride to get to my hometown. I sent a card, and, whenever possible, I called (we didn't have a phone and had to go to the post office or to my husband's aunt to use hers). Invariably, I received a card from my father, with cash inside the envelope and a note telling me to buy myself "something nice." I'm saying all of this to show that my visit home at the end of April in 1983 was something out of the ordinary. Since moving away in 1971 I had gone there only for Christmas or summer vacation. I can't say now what prompted me to go at that particular time. I taught classes in the middle of the week, so I could easily travel on any Friday and return on Monday. Why didn't I go the following weekend in order to be with my parents on Father's name day? Was it because I had to attend some function at the university? Could I have been filled with some uncanny foreboding? No matter how much I speculate, it'll never be more than guesswork.

I have no memory of what we did during the two days we stayed at my parents'. Father's death nullified everything that took place prior to my receiving the news, as if all the memories of the preceding days had to be obliterated to make room for what at once had become most important, commanding my complete attention, my waking hours and dreams. I can only recall that when we were saying our goodbyes, he remarked that they were thinking of coming to see us in June.

We arrived back in Wrocław late Monday evening and immediately went to bed. The next morning we were woken up at six by my husband's aunt, who rang the bell to our apartment. I was surprised to see her so early in the day. I knew something must have happened, but I assumed it had to do with her family. She wasted no time: my mother had called, she said, and asked her to let us know that my father had died. A stroke had caused a brain hemorrhage. I later found out that a few hours after we had left, he started complaining about a headache and got in bed. When my mother went to check on him, she had trouble waking him. He began to mumble something she couldn't understand. Because he'd had a minor stroke before, she immediately phoned for an ambulance. He was taken to the hospital and died before morning. Although his death was completely unexpected, not for a moment did I think that the news couldn't have possibly been true. I accepted the fact of it at once, though I didn't accept his death which cheated me of the years I could have had him around.

If heart-rending news is supposed to transform the surrounding reality into a blur, dimming all sensations except that of pain, it didn't happen to me. My mind instantly went into overdrive, taking in and recording all the minute details, with no selection whatsoever, as though it had turned into a movie camera which someone had forgotten to switch off. I remained in a state of heightened deranged sensitivity for the next few days. I now think it may have been a coping mechanism: the focus on sense perceptions left no room for contemplating the enormity of my loss, the first death of someone I loved.

I didn't go to work that day. The next day I showed up and taught my classes. On the surface I was functional and matter-of-fact, attending to practical matters in what must have looked like a detached and cold-hearted manner. I needed an appropriate outfit. I had a black skirt and black shoes but no proper coat or blouse. It wasn't like I could walk into a store and buy all the necessary items. The shortages were even worse than before. One of my colleagues whose relative lived in Sweden and regularly sent her packages with clothes said she might have a suitable black blouse. I went to her place to see it. It had tiny fake pearls around the neckline, not exactly my style, but I couldn't be choosy. I borrowed a coat from another of my husband's aunts. She was only a bit taller than me.

The day before the funeral we drove to my hometown. The sky was overcast and it was chilly. My husband tried to talk to me, and each time he did, it made me angry. He hadn't lost a father; I had. There was nothing then that could bridge the chasm between us. My emotions were turbulently chaotic and knotted up. I could find no words to express my grief, so I wanted to remain silent. We got to our destination at dusk and went directly to the chapel where the casket was. I stood in front of it but couldn't see Father. It was someone who couldn't have been him, a stranger who pretended to be him, lifeless, cold, the bruised fingers wrapped in a rosary and holding a crucifix, though Father was an atheist. For months afterward, each time I tried to remember him, the only likeness I could summon was that of his body in the coffin, as if my other visual memories of him had been forced out and erased. I looked at his photographs trying to drive the distressing image away, but the minute I closed the picture album, his dead face appeared before my inner eye. Throughout that time I painstakingly worked on conjuring up my earlier memories of him, hoping they would combine into a narrative and give him back to me the way he was in life, and not in death.

RITUALS

After the funeral I wore black for three months. I didn't follow the old rule that a daughter should wear black for one year, but I wanted at least for some time to mark my otherness, my difference from those around me, to announce to the world that I had been singled out and was grieving. Mourning wasn't yet relegated to the private sphere as it is today, when after the funeral, life is supposed to resume, and no one, except the bereaved, should be aware of their loss. Back then some people still wore black for the traditionally required duration and still kept an all night vigil at the dead person's coffin, though younger generations refused to follow the traditional rituals. My family didn't abide by them, either, but it can't be denied that these rituals played an important role. At a time of a loved one's death, when things turned upside down and the world became unhinged, they imposed a sense of order, telling us what was expected and how we should behave. They gave external form to what was hidden, helped express silent grief when words weren't enough, and offered some comfort even if they couldn't alleviate the pain and ultimately you were left alone with it.

CEMETERIES

Until Father's death I didn't have any of my own dead in our local cemetery. All ours were buried elsewhere—in the small village my grandmother came from, in Mława, my maternal grandfather's birthplace or in Lithuania, my father's birthplace. We were fortunate to be spared the deaths of the people in my immediate family, but when I was a child, I wished there was at least one grave in my hometown that belonged to us. I remember how in elementary school I envied those kids who had "their" graves in the cemetery. I felt particularly deprived before All Souls' and All Saints' Days, which were holidays devoted to the remembrance of the dead. Many days before November 1, the cemeteries would fill up with people clearing grave sites, polishing tombstones, placing on them huge pots of white chrysanthemums and candles to be lit on those two days. Although most people in my hometown were newcomers who arrived there after the war, many already had their family graves.

When I was in eighth grade, together with three of my close friends who were in the same predicament, we hit on a brilliant idea. There was a small old German cemetery right in the middle of the town, along its main street. It was neglected since the relatives of the people buried there had fled the area at the end of the war. My friends and I belonged to the girl scouts, and every October we would go there to rake leaves. This time, though, we decided that each of us would adopt several graves, and take care of them as if they belonged to our families. In late October we headed to the cemetery and stayed there working on "our" graves until it got dark. We saved money to buy a potted chrysanthemum for each one. We kept the whole thing a secret, and on November 1, right after church, we went to our graves to light the candles. Later in the day whole families would go to the large municipal cemetery that opened after the war. Even if none of your family members were buried there, you were supposed to go, visit with people you knew, bringing your own candles and lighting them on the graves.

Today when I visit Poland, I always visit my hometown's cemetery. There are now two other graves there besides my father's: my mother's and grandmother's. I clean the gravestones, place flowers in the marble vases, light candles. I'm drawn to cemeteries. Maybe because I'm now more about subtraction than addition, I seek them out wherever I go. It can be a small and modest village graveyard with only a few gravestones or the large and impressive Protestant cemetery in Rome. I stroll around, read the epitaphs, the dates, and count how long the person lived. Do I go there trying to domesticate death? To get a whiff of what Charles Lamb called "the unpalatable draught of mortality"? Possibly. But I also go there to reclaim life. Beyond everything, "Death is the mother of beauty" as Wallace Stevens reminds us in his great poem. Cemeteries have become a metaphysical space in which I contemplate my transience and love of life, my indefiniteness and finality.

FUNERALS

While I was protected against lots of things as a child, no one thought I needed to be protected against familiarity with death. I was often taken to funerals, first to the dead person's home, then to the church, and the cemetery. I heard the adults talk about so-and-so dying, but death's finality was beyond me. Like most young children, I was convinced the dead person would be back soon, alive and well, though Death supposedly cut their heads off. In all the pictures I ever saw of Death, she was depicted as a woman (death is feminine in Polish) carrying a scythe, so each time we attended the viewing, I tried to peek and see the cut the scythe had made on the corpse's neck. My misconception was corrected when I asked my mother how it was possible for the head to be so neatly sewn back to the body that I couldn't see the stitches.

The first funeral I vividly remember was that of my grandmother's best friend, Pani Sabina, who got sick when I was five. I was Grandmother's faithful sidekick, always wanting to do what she did, so I accompanied her many times when she went to see her sick friend. Pani Sabina died the following year. I remember how old I was because I did the math some years later: Grandmother, despairing over her friend's death, kept repeating that she herself had just turned fifty-one, and Sabina, a year younger, was already gone. Her funeral took place on a bleak winter day. We followed the horse-drawn hearse that except for its black color looked to me like Cinderella's carriage in my book of Christian Andersen's fairy tales. I was wearing my warmest coat, but by the time we got to the cemetery, I was shivering from cold and wanted to go home. The priest droned on, and I could see that Grandmother had had enough. I turned around and hid my face in her coat. Then I heard a terrifying sound. The loud thuds of the frozen lumps of dirt thrown on the coffin scared me so badly I burst out crying. Seeing Pani Sabina's dead body in an open coffin beforehand didn't affect me at all. The sounds, though, had such a finality to them that I knew she was gone forever and that death was something awful and irreversible.

When I was in second grade, my schoolmate drowned in the local lake, and most of the students went to her funeral. She lived on a street across the railway tracks from our apartment building, and I would often meet her on the way to school. We walked together and parted ways at the school entrance because she was one grade above mine. Sometimes I'd see her after lessons, and I'd accompany her all the way to the railway crossing where she'd continue straight on and I'd turn left and head home. I don't remember what we talked about, but I remember that I liked her. One day in winter I heard she had drowned the day before. She was skating on the frozen lake where all of us skated when she went too close to where the river Drwęca flowed into it. The ice there was thin, and it broke under her weight. Everyone at the school was talking about the accident. I couldn't stop thinking of the freezing cold water sucking her under the ice, of her feet with heavy boots and skates that pulled her down like weights. She must have been screaming or maybe her voice was stuck in her throat. I kept re-imagining her drowning, coming up with more and more scary details. Before the funeral I went to her home, my first visit there. My friend lay in a white coffin in her first communion dress tied at the waist with a golden-brown rope. Her fingers were bruised, and so was her face.

Her death was the first death of a young person I knew. Until then I had gone to the funerals of older people who died of old age or sickness. Their deaths didn't disturb me because they didn't disturb the order of the world I took for granted. But my friend's death caused me deep anguish. My life too could be snatched from me. Kids weren't safe since one's youth offered no protection against death. It was enough to take one wrong step and not pay attention. I wouldn't have been able to put my feelings into words; they were just a vague sensation, yet on some subliminal level I knew that chance and randomness ruled the world. My friend had been here just a few days before, walking to school with me, and then, suddenly and with no warning, she was gone. For a long time after her funeral I was ridden with anxiety. I became exceedingly cautious. I took forever to cross the street. That winter I never skated on the lake.

SUICIDE

Suicide provoked both private pity and public opprobrium. No one talked openly about it. Families were ashamed, and the mourners didn't know how to behave: should they offer condolences for the person who chose not to go on living? If families could have hidden suicide, they would have done so. An overdose of sleeping pills or a jump off the tenth floor could be explained as honest mistakes, but in my small hometown such opportunities didn't exist. Most deaths by suicide were obvious. People hanged themselves or put their heads in the oven, turning on the gas. Our next door neighbor killed himself by drinking hydrochloric acid. I had no idea that his death was suicide until many years later. I was too young to be told that sometimes people took their own lives. When we went to the neighbor's apartment for the viewing, I saw that his face was covered with a white cloth, but it didn't occur to me to ask questions. Everyone else knew how he had died, and he was buried in the unconsecrated part of the cemetery since the Catholic church condemned suicide. He suspected his wife was having an affair. He came home drunk late at night, and when his wife refused to let him in, he drank the acid standing before their front door, convinced her lover was there with her. Why he brought a jar of acid from work, nobody knew. He couldn't have planned to kill himself, people were saying, in such a horrible way. He would have come up with a better method.

One fall when I was in high school, the whole town was abuzz. Two young men who were good friends hanged themselves from trees in a local park a week apart. Everyone pronounced it a suicide pact and thought others would follow. After the second death the police began to patrol the park, and things quieted down. There was widespread speculation, none conclusive, as to why such young men with their whole lives before them had decided to commit suicide. Some years earlier I might have viewed suicide as romantic, particularly if it was committed by a spurned lover or an artist who decided to end his life because of ennui and existential dissatisfaction with the world. By the time those two suicides happened I had already read *Madame Bovary* with its gruesome graphic description of Emma Bovary's suicidal death. I knew there was nothing romantic about someone taking his own life. Those two suicides occurred almost on my doorstep. I often saw one of the men walking the streets with his German shepherd, so I knew him by sight. He looked to me like a Viking, blond and handsome. A few times I was even tempted to ask if I could pet his dog, but at the last moment I got cold feet. Years later, reading Sándor Márai's *Diary*, I remembered that suicide. Márai says that death doesn't come from outside, that it is within us, completely within us. One day we find it like we find something in the pocket of our winter coat. That image has never left me. Márai found his when he bought a pistol and trained himself to shoot.

MY DEAD

Mother died two months before she would have turned sixty-three. If deaths can be divided into good and bad, hers didn't belong to the former category. She had amyotrophic lateral sclerosis. Widowed for several years, she had re-married, and her new husband took care of her, which was a blessing, since I could visit only in the summer. Fortunately, too, my sister and her family lived in a neighboring city as did my mother's sister. A friend's mother had died of ALS a few years after we graduated from the university, so I was familiar with the disease and knew there was no cure. Its slow but irrevocable progress imparted bitter and painful knowledge about the terrible desolation and loneliness of the dying. Mother was surrounded by family, but she had crossed over to the territory we had no access to, and she was aware of her separateness from us. Even when she was well, she'd rarely talked about herself and was never inclined to share confidences. Our bond wasn't based on talking. She just was there, did things for me and my sister, gave me books, went to teacher-parent meetings, but she kept thoughts to herself, and by the time I was a teenager I carefully skirted the demarcations she had created. I knew much less about her childhood and youth than I did about that of my father and grandmother who were both gregarious storytellers. I always hoped, though, that one day we would talk and that I would find out how she felt and what she thought.

Our final visit with her took place in July. At the time I didn't know I'd never see her again. I somehow convinced myself that she'd be around much longer. While we all knew she was terminally ill, none of us talked to her about it. I wanted to but was afraid even to try. Such topics were off limits in our family. The only thing I heard her say was, "I'm not afraid to die. I just don't like this dying." While I was prepared for Mother's death—as far as one can ever be prepared for a loved one's passing—the experience was much more trau-matic than it should have been according to the common lore on the subject. If we go through anticipatory grief, we should be able to cope with death more easily. I didn't. Father died suddenly, and I grieved a long time, but ultimately with few regrets. I had more sense of him as a person, and my relation-ship with him was more fully developed. After Mother's death I was ridden with unabated remorse and guilt. We never had the heart-to-heart mother-daughter talk I so much wanted to have and never would.

For my grandmother, Mother's death was a great injustice. Providence had failed her by letting her outlive her daughter. She was too old to rebel against God or Fate, but she couldn't come to terms with the tragedy. A child's death, no matter the age, is always a tragedy for the parent. And for a mother, in particular, a child remains a child forever. Medieval artists knew that very well: the paintings of the *Pietà corpusculum* show Mary holding an adult Christ the size of a child.

Grandmother herself died a good death. She slowly faded and died in her sleep. Her longtime prayer or rather supplication to Death which I heard her say—"You who walk with a scythe come barefoot at night"—was answered. She lived to be almost ninety-four, but she'd been on familiar terms with death for many years prior. She was convinced she'd die at sixty-seven as both her parents died at that age, and she believed in genetic determination. Because of this conviction, she stoically prepared everything to make sure her wishes would be followed. When the year passed and she turned sixty-eight, she thought she'd gotten a year's respite. Eventually, she had to admit that her calculations were wrong. Despite the evidence to the contrary—she remained in good health for many years—she continued, partly in jest, to plan her funeral. Never vain, she intended to look elegant for her last exit, and every few years changed her mind about the dress she wanted to be buried in. All her plans and preparations were for the benefit of the living who would witness her grand departure. She seemed not to worry about any other baggage, spiritual or material, that might accompany her into the afterlife.

None of my family members cared in any way about memorializing themselves. Father's death was sudden, but even if he had had a premonition, he wouldn't have bothered about what he'd be leaving for posterity. None kept a journal, and the only material objects that prove they were alive are photographs, all of which would fit into a shoe box. Did they trust they would be preserved in the memory of the family members who survived them? They probably counted on our learning from their example since they themselves were such reliable keepers of our family's memories.

*

With both my parents and grandmother gone, my last buffer has disappeared. I am now closer to my dead than ever before, and their ranks have expanded with the deaths of close friends. My memory continues to evoke them, but how much of it is re-creation of the way they really were and how much invention? Are they still themselves or are they losing their identity and becoming me after they pass through the crucible of my memory?

These days they constantly remind me of their absent presence. They enter my dreams with less ceremony than in the past, sensing that they can live more fully here than in my waking hours when I know they're forever gone. They visit me as though their own eternal sleep weren't enough, and they needed to steal some of mine. After I wake, they refuse to leave, and I carry them with me throughout the day and into the next night.

AFLOAT

Swimmers can be divided into those who hold their head above water and never put their face down, those who in order to swim must feel the ground under their feet, those who always wear caps and goggles, those who swim only in indoor pools, those who love salt water, those who definitely prefer lakes, and those who have decided to try to outdo today's runners (who constantly talk about running) by talking about swimming. I'd go on with the classification if I weren't afraid I'd end up with something Borgesian. Suffice it to say I belong to the final two categories, although my membership in the last one only began when I decided to write this piece.

*

In 2005 I had Lasik surgery to correct my terrible near-sightedness. Like most people who have to wear glasses, I was looking forward to being free of them. Glasses, though, weren't the sole or even the most important reason for my decision, though that was the explanation I gave to anyone who asked. The truth was I wanted to be able to see while swimming. I realize this sounds bizarre. How much sight does a swimmer need? Besides, aren't there prescription goggles that can make you see clearly? That's all correct if we're talking about swimming in a pool. But I am an outdoor, lake swimmer, and goggles and other paraphernalia don't belong in my swimming universe. I don't I like pools because I feel trapped in their enclosed space, boxed in by the lanes where you have to be careful not to hit the ropes, and I feel imposed upon by a sudden urge to count. Swimming in a pool deprives me of freedom, which for me has always been what swimming is all about.

*

My family usually went to the municipal beach on the large Drwęckie Lake, which jutted into our town. There were life-guards on duty, and a pier demarcated the area where one was allowed to swim. It was a crowded place, and you had to arrive early if you wanted to get a changing cabin and then secure a good spot for your blanket, which meant sunny and shady at the same time. Not that children spent much time on those family blankets. The minute we got to the beach and took our clothes off, we ran to the water. Mothers would urge us to remember to come and get a bite, but none of us listened. Around lunchtime they would resignedly leave the blankets and search for their kids in the lake. We'd hear them yelling "Marysia, come here right this minute," but when our own names were called, we pretended not to hear until an adult threatened to get in the water and drag out the recalcitrant offender. We wolfed down lunch, usually sandwiches with butter that had melted in the heat, a hard-boiled egg, a tomato or a half-sour pickle. During the strawberry season, we'd eat mushy strawberries out of a juice-soaked paper sack that used to have sugar in it, and later in the summer bruised pears or tart gooseberries with fuzzy skin. But finishing the food didn't mean we could run back to the water. The accepted wisdom was that one wasn't supposed to swim after a meal for at least thirty minutes. That half hour was torture. Since most people would usually head home around 5 pm, the time after lunch could be spent blissfully in the lake. When the final call came, we all looked like corpses that had been pulled out of water. Our teeth chattered, our skin was wrinkled, we had goose bumps all over, and we looked pasty and wan as if a particularly bloodthirsty vampire had drunk our blood.

The other beach we went to was called "wild," the label referring to its illegitimate character. At the beginning of each summer there was a "No Swimming" sign next to the water, but within a few days it was gone and didn't re-appear until the next year. The beach was beautiful. To get to it, you had to cross the cemetery with the graves of the Soviet soldiers who were killed at the end of WWII while liberating our town. Then you walked in a long alley shaded by two rows of maple trees. When you saw a municipal cemetery on your left, you knew you were close. A few hundred meters and you could hear the happy sounds from the beach. The lake was at the bottom of the hill which back then seemed like a mountain to me. I loved nothing more than to stop at the top and look down. I pretended it was the lake from the movie *Treasure in a Silver Lake* with the brave Appachee chief Winnetou and his friend Old Shatterhand. I was the heroine who bravely swam in it with her beloved. Before beginning my descent, I took my shoes off. The hill was sandy, and at the top the sand was mixed with dirt, but as you went down it became warm and uniformly gold, much nicer than the sand at the municipal beach.

I loved that lake because unlike at the other one there were no lifeguards. I could swim out and no one—unless I was there with my parents—would yell at me to stay close to the shore. Each year we heard of people drowning there. The story went that there were dangerous whirlpools which sucked in even experienced swimmers. I was cautious at first but eventually ignored the warnings, and in my teens I regularly swam across to the other side and back. Fortunately, the lake was too small for motorboats, so only an occasional kayak or canoe would appear on it.

*

I learned to swim by imitation the way most children of my generation did. I grew up in the area of Poland that was grandiloquently called "The Land of a Thousand Lakes," and summer swimming in a lake belonged to my childhood rituals the way skiing belongs to them if you spend your youth in a mountainous region. I remember my father holding me in the water while I tried to copy the movements of the breast-stroke my mother had shown me. Both my parents were poor swimmers, and I quickly figured out that the best way to learn was by watching those more advanced than I. When at last I managed to lift my legs off the bottom while doing a furious dog paddle, I knew I was onto something wonderful. I discovered that if I lay flat on my back, the water would keep me afloat and I could rest staring at the sky. Soon I could do the breaststroke, holding my head stiffly above the water, but it wasn't until the following summer when I began to put my whole face in the water and breathe out bubbles of air that I felt really accomplished.

My early attempts at swimming underwater were pathetic. I had to hold my nose squeezed tight between my thumb and index finger and close my eyes to jump in. A big breakthrough happened when I learned to do it with my nose unplugged and eyes open. Soon I held my breath for quite a while, a feat which let me explore the bottom of the lake at its shallower end. This murky underwater world of permanent dusk was both alluring and scary, a rich realm for imagination. I peopled it with mermaids and benign water creatures, but it also had its darker side: slimy branches of fallen trees that could grab and clutch you like a drowned person's hands, the mazes of weeds that oozed out turbid residue and could entangle you forever.

When I was eleven or so I saw in our local theater a Russian movie whose Polish title was *The Sea Devil*. It was a science fiction film, black and white, but at the time I wouldn't have known its genre. It was also a love story. For me, however, the most interesting part had to do with the male protagonist's father, an eminent scientist, who implanted a shark's gills into his son's chest. The son could breathe with his lungs, but they were weak, and the surgery allowed him to spare them. Although he could stay for periods of time on land, he preferred underwater existence. I still remember how taken I was with the shots of his swimming deep in the sea. I loved to pretend that instead of lungs I also had shark's gills and was no longer an intruder in the parallel world I found so enticing.

In my teens I turned into an adroit swimmer. As my breathing became coordinated with my head going in and out of water, swimming got easy and I could cover long stretches without feeling tired. I was no good at PE and hated it when I had to vault the horse or do plain calisthenics. When we played ball, I was afraid the ball would hit me in the face. I wasn't competitive in sports, and team effort just wasn't for me. The only thing I wanted was for the misery to be over. I also disliked getting sweaty and later having to put my regular clothes back on to attend other classes since the school had no proper gym facilities.

Swimming was different. It gave me numerous psychological compensations for my poor athletic performance. I was never clumsy when I swam. I easily befriended my body. My movements were fluid and smooth, and I often felt as if I had no body, a desirable condition for a teenage girl who viewed herself in the mirror with merciless criticism. When I swam far out into a lake, with water covering me and only my head bobbing, I was powerful and invisible, the state I often wished for during my PE classes. I didn't have to watch others and envy their dexterity. Even when I swam with friends, I never associated swimming with competition or treated it like a sport. I had no other goal except to swim. But I liked it best when I swam alone and could daydream undisturbed. The only sounds I could hear were my breathing and the lapping water.

Don't get me wrong, I was by no means a loner. I had a group of close friends with whom I spent a lot of time, but early on I discovered that I also loved solitude. It was a pity the Polish climate prevented me from swimming year round. All the adults kept saying that the proper time to begin was June 24, the date that coincided with the end of the school year. As I got older, I ignored the warnings about getting in the lake before it had time to warm up properly. I intrepidly swam in such cold water that the only way to overcome my body's resistance was to rush in as quickly as possible. The soonest I ever did it was in mid May when my friends and I went on a picnic to one of the lakes hidden deep in the woods near our hometown. The water was freezing cold as if the ice had barely melted on it. All of us had planned to swim, but my friends gave up after dipping their feet in. Maybe to make up for my customary PE flops, I decided to impress them with my dauntlessness. The minute I went in, I knew I was a fool as the coldness literally took my breath away. I wouldn't turn back, though, even if I were to die of pneumonia, a likely consequence of my desire to show off. I began swimming freestyle, the best stroke to propel me swiftly forward and make me feel less cold. In a few minutes I was all right and continued my vigorous motions a while longer. Even now I get chills when I recall that incident.

My fear of PE continued in college. To escape the dreaded class, which I had to take for two semesters, I decided to try out for the swim team. I made it, and three times a week I had to show up for a 6:30am practice at the pool. At that time the university used the pool in the old public bathhouse, close to a tram stop. Riding the early tram full of sulky passengers on their way to work (yes, the normal work hours under communism were 7am to 3pm), I often had second thoughts, but once I entered the bathhouse whose interior was suffused in misty steam, I was proud I had dragged myself out of bed at the ungodly hour in order to swim. As I said earlier, I wasn't a fan of pools, but swimming beat the ordeal of a regular PE class. We swam laps, the coach corrected us and timed us, and within thirty minutes we were done. Since we had no goggles and the water was heavily chlorinated, I developed a bad case of conjunctivitis. I got better when I stayed away from the pool, but the moment I returned, my eyes again looked like those of an albino rabbit. At last I went to an eye doctor, an older man, most likely retired from his regular job and supplementing his income with a few hours at the university clinic. No one was in the waiting room so he took his time talking with me. I told him I majored in English. He said that English was beyond him. He only spoke German and French. I confided in him my dislike of PE. He said he'd excuse me for a while from the swim team. He wrote something on a sheet of paper, stamped it with his seal to make it officially valid, and handed it to me. I didn't look at it until I was downstairs. I couldn't believe my good fortune: due to poor health I was released from both the swim team and PE for the whole academic year.

*

After swimming for years in California's manmade reservoirs, I'm swimming at last in a real lake—actually a pond, Walden Pond—though it's the size of a lake and it smells the way my childhood lakes did. In New England, where we have now lived for a few years, that label is reserved for those bodies of water that have tributaries. Right now linguistic sophistry is the furthest thing from my mind. I'm having the time of my life even if that statement is something of an exaggeration. I push my arms forward, breathe in, go under, breathe out, emerge, the rhythm easy and natural. No other activity makes us enter an alien element the way swimming does, where we leave air and submerge ourselves in a much thicker substance that makes us forget our solidity. We float in utero, and babies can swim from right after birth till they're about six months old. Though we soon forget our fish-like ability and have to re-learn the skill we were born with, the desire to return to our aquatic beginnings is still very strong.

I do the breaststroke swimming out. My mind has emptied itself, my body dissolving in water, the act of swimming indistinguishable from *me* swimming, the feeling of bound-lessness—the closest I can ever get to the foretaste of infinity. I love the sensuality of being enveloped in liquid, each part of my body touched and caressed. In the middle of the lake I lie flat on the water watching the drama of the clouds and inhaling the smells. Tactile sensations aren't the only sensual pleasures of swimming. Lakes have their peculiar odors, so strong that the surrounding air is imbued with them. I can be some distance away and my nose will tell me that I'm approaching a lake, and when I lie motionless on the water, the smells are so intense that they upstage all other sensations.

After this serenely Zen moment I turn back. I see my husband standing at the edge of the water and waving for me to return. He's no swimmer, so each time I swim far away from the shore, he worries I'll drown. I tease him a bit, dive and stay underwater.

The gates to nowhere multiply . . .
　　　　—Mark Strand "Bury Your Face in Your Hands"

THE DISPLACED

I knew the outer you and some facts. But facts alone won't reveal the truth, the inner truth of a life. If it's difficult to reclaim even my own past, fill in the blanks on my own life's map, how can I do it for you? I can only chase you with words. Writing about the dead isn't any easier than writing about a living person, as no life is ever complete even when it's over. Nothing is as impalpable as another human being.

When I found out about your death, I was weighted with emotion and grieved for you like I would for someone very close to me. You haunted me. Yes, *haunted* is the right word as for the longest time you kept returning in my thoughts and refused to leave. Was it because I sensed a kinship between us, identified with you, thought I dodged what broke you, and felt a retrospective selfish fear for myself? I asked questions that had no answers. Could your life have turned out differently? Could someone or something have arrested your downward slide? Time passed and, as usually happens, I finally stopped thinking of what had occurred that summer.

Until now, that is, almost twenty years since you died.

Some events from the past return in strange and unpredictable ways. A few weeks ago I was looking for Anne Fadiman's *Ex Libris* and *At Large and At Small*. I was feeling down after the excitement of my three-month stay in Kraków. I wanted to read something that in the past invariably boosted my spirits. My thorough search of our bookcases yielded nothing. The books had vanished. I must have loaned them to someone, and they never found their way back. Not to waste any more time, I went to Amazon and typed in Anne Fadiman's name. The book that appeared at the top of the list was *The Spirit Catches You and You Fall Down*. I hadn't read it, but I was familiar with the title. I told myself that I should get it together with the other two. I lived in the Central Valley for twenty-one years; Merced, where the book is set, is a nearby town. I also had quite a few Hmong students at the college where I used to teach before we moved to Massachusetts. I scrolled down, and the third item was something called *Quicklet—Anne Fadiman's The Spirit Catches You*. I had no idea what a quicklet was, but its author's name stopped me. It was your last name. I clicked on the link, and saw a short bio: the writer was a native of Merced. That only confirmed what I already suspected: your older son wrote it. This chance occurrence was like a postscript from you.

Certain memories can be easily brought back as if they were floating on the surface of consciousness. Others need help if they're to emerge from the shadows. I started looking at pictures in my photo albums and found one with you, not a portrait, just a group picture from a Polish Christmas party. It was the first time we met. We're standing next to each other. I'm holding my younger daughter, a white hand towel over my shoulder, to keep the baby from messing up my red dress. You're wearing a black dress and holding a plastic cup with red wine in it. We both have shoulder-length hair, yours blonde, mine dark.

Right behind you I see your husband, a head taller than you, in a navy blue suit, a blue shirt and a purple tie, sporting a beard and a moustache, his glasses lens reflecting the overhead light. In his arms he has your two-year-old son. Your older son stands in front of you in blue jeans and a white t-shirt with the Sea World logo. Both boys have flaxen hair, lighter than yours. Almost everyone in the picture grins, showing their teeth; we had all learned to smile the American way.

Your husband, handsome, sharp-witted and smooth-talking, could make a good impression. He was charming despite brief flashes of arrogance. After we were introduced, almost at once he announced his attachment to America, calling it the best place in the world. His sons were born here, so each could advance and maybe even run for president. When he said that to me, I thought he was being facetious. But he wasn't joking. He was sober, serious, and sincere. I wondered later why he delivered this pronouncement to me. Did he try to set me right because he'd heard from other Poles that I wasn't America's apologist and despised Ronald Reagan, whom most of them worshipped? Or was it a pre-emptive gambit he typically used with fellow Americans in case they entertained some doubt about his belonging to the desirable emigrants in love with their new country? Had he forgotten that I was not one of them?

The same evening he filled me in on how the two of you had met.

He was in a medical residency in one of the Chicago hospitals. A fellow doctor from India told him that his family had a new nanny, a pretty Polish woman who spoke flawless English. He suggested that his colleague, a single man, meet her. He offered to invite both of you to dinner at his house. Your future husband had met the colleague's wife before, a charming woman but quite overweight. He concluded that he and his friend probably subscribed to different standards of female attractiveness. Not wanting to be discourteous, he accepted his colleague's invitation. When he met you, he had to admit that the Indian doctor was right. You were beautiful, witty, and smart. He was smitten. He started asking you out.

You and I attended many gatherings like the one at which we met, but I have no more photos. We had some things in common: our age—you were one year younger than I; two young children; MA's in English literature—yours from the Jagiellonian University in Kraków, mine from the University of Wrocław. We came from small towns: you from the south of Poland, I from the northeast. Each of us had been previously married and divorced. Like me, you liked to read poetry, but unlike me, you also wrote it. I sensed that you, too, didn't quite belong with that group of Polish immigrants. In our conversations we never broached the subject of our lives in Poland, as if it was something that should be left alone and not revisited. We played it safe, focused on the present, skimming the surfaces of our lives, sharing public personas. We were friendly acquaintances who didn't become friends the way a Polish person would define friendship. Neither of us took the necessary steps, neither broke out of the self-imposed reserve, though given our affinities, it would have been the most natural thing.

The previous year my family had moved to Fresno for my husband's new job. The city, despite its size, seemed a depressing backwater. That fall, thanks to my newly obtained green card, I had started teaching part-time at the university. After a series of discouraging dealings with the INS, I was thrilled to have a job. But we couldn't afford daycare or babysitters for our two young daughters, and I often felt overwhelmed, exhausted, and dispirited. After living for four years in two university towns in Virginia and North Carolina, moving to California's Central

Valley was like another immigration for me. I met some of my husband's colleagues but made no friends of my own. I had a hard time getting used to the alien space and climate, which were so different from anything I had experienced before: the parched fields, the layer of dust covering the trees, the brutal sun with summer temperatures soaring to 110 degrees F, and in late fall and winter the tule fog that enveloped everything. I painfully felt my estrangement and thought I had fallen into a limbo I would never exit.

You, on the other hand, seemed to have mastered all the ins and outs of American life. Your life appeared carefully assembled, well-lived, enviable. You were about to finish the graduate program in linguistics at Cal State, Fresno. An American university diploma would open more doors than a Polish MA alone. I saw you as well adjusted and self-sufficient, and I aspired to your ease and confidence. I assumed you had many friends in Merced and didn't need anyone else. You had arrived in this country several years before I did and lived in California for quite a while. Those extra years, I told myself, gave you an edge. It was just a question of time. Things were bound to fall into place for me too.

There was nothing in your demeanor that would make me question my impression of you. It never crossed my mind that you might have wanted everyone to see the decorous, scrupulously maintained facade. You didn't intend to deceive. I must have created a similar impression. By nature an introvert, I too hid quite well. That's how it works. We both wore protective armor for fear that we might expose our vulnerability. We wanted others to see the light, not the shadows. Maybe showing the bright optimistic version was the first sign of our Americanization.

You came to America in a year of turmoil and uncertainty in Poland, marked by workers' strikes and the inception of the Solidarity movement. Although on August 31, 1980 the government was forced to sign an agreement with striking workers and thereby accept the existence of a free trade union, the exhilaration at the news was tainted with skepticism. Almost no one believed that the Party would honor the deal in the long run. Daily life was as hard as ever, the shortages that had beset our lives worse than before. That summer I was in Berlin where I worked illegally. There was a real chance of Soviet intervention in Poland. Like so many other Poles who happened to be abroad, I wondered if I shouldn't consider immigration. But I didn't see myself living elsewhere. After two months I went back. Four years later I left for Virginia as an exchange visitor. At the university there I met my American husband.

I don't know the exact date of your arrival in Chicago. I do know that in the early 1980s an American visa must have looked to you like a lifeline. You were sick of the precariousness and unpredictability of our lives, and of politics casting a long shadow on all our doings. Like so many others, you craved what we referred to as "a normal life," which was lived by people in other countries but denied to us. Procuring most basic products like meat and detergent, and hustling from one private English lesson to another to make ends meet—that was your life, most of it wasted on pedestrian concerns, with little time left for anything else. You began to dream of leaving, of giving yourself a break, since you didn't know if you'd be able to stay for good or would want to. The natural place to go to was America whose myth was suddenly more alluring than ever. Your English was getting rusty, you claimed. You could work in America and bring back some money. That's what you told everyone, including your husband. You kept to yourself one other reason for wanting to escape. Your marriage had grown stale, maybe a casualty of your humdrum existence.

The decision to move to another place is invariably colored with optimism. A new place entices with the promise of a new beginning. Most of us like new beginnings. We tend to think they might let us shed our old skin and become someone we always wanted to be. This, though, isn't entirely true and belongs in the realm of wishful thinking. Doubtless there's change involved when we have to face new challenges and situations, but we carry our old selves with us wherever we go. They, like culture and upbringing, cannot be discarded. You knew all that. You desired change in your outward circumstances which could enlarge or corrode the self, but in the manner of most potential immigrants you hoped that new conditions would bring about the expansion of your mind and spirit. When making the decision to move, we don't want to deprive ourselves of the beautiful illusion that everything, including our inner selves, will be richer and better. Without that fiction we might stay put and never attempt to escape.

So you came to Chicago, and soon after, you got a nanny's job with the Indian doctor's family. You met the ambitious Polish doctor who'd earned his degree from the Warsaw Medical Academy and was finishing up his residency in order to be able to practice in America. He was five years older than you, a good conversationalist, tall and handsome. You fell in love; you no longer thought of going back. If you hesitated at all, the Declaration of Martial Law on December 13, 1981 was a clincher, just as it was for so many other Poles who happened to be away.

Your new husband got a job offer, and your future looked bright. You knew nothing about the San Joaquin Valley before you moved there. I wonder if back in Chicago, a great cosmopolitan city, with an array of cultural events, theater, movies, art galleries, and an international crowd, you had any inkling that you would end up in a rural area where life was slow paced and uneventful. But a small town may have promised just the kind of normality you longed for in Poland. You'd have time to write poems; you'd meet interesting locals—there were bound to be some; you'd gladly make do with what was there; you'd be happy. So even if the town you settled in had struck you as provincial, you wanted to like it. It couldn't be compared to Kraków or Chicago, yet it had its assets. It was only two hours away from Yosemite, a short drive from the Pacific coast, and San Francisco was within reach. You had a large house shaded by trees, with a swimming pool, in a peaceful area, a perfect place to raise the children you planned to have. You must have been excited to have so much space after the crowded quarters we occupied in Poland. In the spring of 1983 you gave birth to your first son; four years later your second son was born. Children would help you feel connected to the unfamiliar place. You would forge and accumulate potent new memories which would take precedence over the old ones.

Some time after we first met, at one of the festivities we were invited to, you asked me about my teaching job. You wanted to start looking for work. I tried to help. I talked to a friend of ours, chair of the English department at a nearby community college. He told me they were always looking for part-time teachers and that my friend should get in touch. You did. I remember your visit to our house before your job interview. You wanted to get some pointers from me. A few days later you called me, excited: You'd been offered two classes. Soon afterwards another phone call followed: you wouldn't be able to take the job. You wanted to apologize to me as if you had let me down. Your husband had an inefficient office manager, and you had to take over to straighten things out. There was something in your voice I hadn't heard before. You tried to sound upbeat, but I detected a trace of dejection. Could you have harbored it earlier and it just didn't register with me?

I didn't say anything to you, but I was baffled. Why wouldn't your husband hire another office manager? I couldn't see you working in a medical office, shuffling papers, organizing files, sending out insurance claims and bills. The tedium and monotony of such a job would have unhinged me. Then, who knows? Maybe you didn't mind. Maybe you wanted to help your husband. You felt bad announcing your decision because of my efforts on your behalf, and I may have misconstrued it as despondency. After that phone conversation, you never called me again, and I never called you. We drifted apart, and our paths didn't cross.

I began to decline invitations to the Polish parties, and you were absent from the few I went to. By then I had made friends at work, met people with similar interests. I also discovered a passion which brought me great pleasure and satisfaction: I began to translate fiction and poetry, something I knew I wouldn't have done if I hadn't left Poland. I realized I didn't have to belong to a place to be contented if other aspects of my life were rewarding. I began to question the whole idea of roots, admitting that in some sense I had always felt rootless.

Even though I withdrew from the Polish community, I remained in loose contact with some of the Polish women and occasionally met them for lunch. At one of those lunches your name came up. Until then I hadn't thought of you for quite some time. One of the women told us that her husband, an economics professor, lectured as a visiting professor at an up and coming business school in a town in southern Poland. You'd asked him if the school needed English teachers and he promised to find out. Your MA degree in linguistics from an American university and his personal recommendation were enough to get you a visiting lecturer job. You planned to take your sons with you. I'm not sure now whether you intended to teach there one or two semesters, not that it matters. I took note of this bit of information but didn't dwell on it.

A few months after that, at another lunch, I found out that you had given up the idea. What happened, I asked the women? Your husband didn't want the boys going with you, one of them said, and you didn't want to leave them. Another woman corrected that, saying that your husband opposed the whole idea to begin with and was against your going even by yourself. This particular woman disapproved of your plans. Your husband, she maintained, was right to put his foot down. Why in the world would you want to go teach in Poland? What were you looking for? You should appreciate your carefree life here. Two great children, a big house, a pool, your husband such a good provider. You didn't even have to work. What else did you want?

I don't know which of the versions was true. Possibly neither one. I can only assume that at least for some time you really wished to go since you went into the trouble of making all the arrangements, just as a few years earlier you wanted to teach at a community college. It's possible your husband had nothing to do with it. You yourself may have decided to stay. What good would one or two semesters in Poland do? You'd still be coming back to your old new life.

You never contemplated going and not returning. You once left your hometown for Kraków, and then Kraków for Chicago. But this time a rift appeared which didn't exist when you first left. There was no continuity between then and now as if your previous life had been wiped out. This time everything was different. Alternatives got canceled because your circumstances changed: you were older, you had two children you loved more than anything. The exit gates closed. Besides, how many times in a lifetime can one try to escape? Going back to Poland for good would mean admitting defeat. Poland had freed itself of Communism and was now a democracy, but any Polish person would tell you that only a loser would leave the comforts and security of American life for a country in the throes of a painful transition to democracy and market capitalism. You didn't want your Polish family and friends to view you as failure. You wanted them to think you were living the

American dream, even though your dreams had abandoned you.

Sometimes you thought about your life back in Poland. It's a terrible irony that we want to leave a place and then begin to miss it because the new place can give us only so much. Places are both physical and metaphysical and without people we feel close to, they can't acquire the metaphysical dimension, indispensable to our sense of well-being and fulfillment. Even the most introverted among us need others. You used to live among friends, among those with whom you shared the past, to whom you didn't have to explain everything because they understood without having to be told.

Now you were isolated and lonely.

You led this perfectly normal life: cooking, shopping, waiting for your sons to come back from school, going to parent-teacher conferences. You drove them to school and extracurricular activities; you picked them up. You helped them with homework. Your husband worked long hours, and when he returned home, you served him dinner. You no longer managed his office, so you could have looked for another job. But you didn't. You must have thought that you had burned your bridges and that it was too late, five or six years after you got your graduate degree. You accused yourself of ingratitude. You had all the comforts one could dream of, and yet you felt bereft. The fault was all yours. You hadn't tried hard enough. You met some of your husband's colleagues from his medical practice, and you met their families. You went to parties at their homes; you gave parties at yours. You dreamed of belonging. But even when you tried, it didn't work. You didn't know what to say, what questions to ask. You never mastered the art of small talk. Your husband couldn't understand. There was a flaw in you. You no longer knew who you were. You felt diminished, displaced. In another life, which didn't seem like yours anymore, you knew who you were. Now you were nobody.

In the fall of 1996 I got a full-time job at a community college. I was busy teaching, translating, mothering our two daughters, with little time to spare. I mention this because that whole year is like a blur, and that's why I'm unsure when I heard about your stay at the local psychiatric hospital. It must have been in the spring because I later reflected on how quickly all the events had mounted up.

What follows is hearsay. Your husband, it was said, had taken you there because you tried to set the house on fire and he was worried about the safety of your sons. Since he couldn't have you committed, he may have demanded that you go for an evaluation and you agreed. You were released after a few days, clearly not deemed dangerous to yourself or others. You denied your husband's accusation. You were distracted, you said. You placed a dish covered with aluminum foil in the microwave and went to another room to check on your sons. When you returned, the microwave and the kitchen cabinet were on fire. I was relieved to hear that. I couldn't bring myself to believe that you would have wanted to harm your children. After you returned from the hospital, you moved into your own apartment. Your sons stayed with your husband. No one knew if it was your decision or if your husband didn't want you around and insisted that you leave.

In the summer of 1997 we didn't go to Poland. We usually traveled there every other year, and that was a year we vacationed in the US. We returned home to Fresno some time at the beginning of August. I remember the stifling heat. I was sitting at the kitchen table watching blue jays in our back yard when a Polish friend called. She asked me if I had heard. Heard what, I said.

You spent your days alone in the furnished apartment you had moved to. You brought only your clothes and a few books. There was nothing there that was yours, no recognizable sounds or smells, no plants you took such loving care of, no stains on the sofa that would make you remember the red wine you had spilled. Your sons would visit you. You were happy to see them. Their visits were your only diversion. There was a TV set that you didn't watch but turned on now and then to drown the silence. You'd go shopping for food, though you had lost your appetite. On some days you'd walk around the apartment complex in the evening when the outdoor heat let up. You'd walk until you wearied yourself. Did you consider a future? Or did you see none, expecting nothing, not waiting for anything because you had nothing to wait for? You were empty inside, hollowed out. It wasn't anything that happened in that apartment that tipped the scales for you and made you think of the only way out. You didn't want to abandon your sons, you loved them, but they'd already been taken away from you. When they came to see you, they couldn't fail to sense your desolation, particularly the older one who was already fourteen, even though you had tried to put on a bright face. What could a person like you give others except her pain? You didn't want them tainted with your despair. You wanted them to grow up and feel that this was their home, their place. You were their mother only in name. They would be better off without you.

You'd been prescribed sleeping pills to help with your insomnia. Now you began to save them. You needed a great many to make sure your plan didn't miscarry. You also bought a big bottle of vodka. Your research showed that alcohol would intensify the effect of the pills. You were very methodical, not leaving anything to chance. A plastic bag would ensure that you wouldn't survive. You had to make your last escape work.

Your older son came to visit you. He saw your car in the parking lot, so he knew you must be inside. He rang the bell several times, then knocked and banged the door. He got worried. When he went to the administrative office, the apartment manager told him to wait there while he went to check. He must have suspected that something was badly amiss.

The circumstances of someone's death usually stay hidden. But when the death is suicide, they become the subject of intense conjecture, speculation, and rumor. Suddenly there's a story to tell. But it's not the story of your death that compelled me to write about you. Anne Fadiman's book and the quicklet your son wrote were obvious triggers, yet the urge came from elsewhere, from somewhere deeper. All along, whenever your name came up, I wanted to believe you were all right. Even after the episode that led to the mental hospital, I convinced myself there was a future for you. I had no intimation that loneliness had turned your life into a desert. I didn't seek information about you—uncertainty offers a kind of solace. Our lives converged for only a very short time. Mine followed a more fortunate course. Was it chance and factors beyond my control that let me leave behind the tangle of my early life here? I found a niche within the unfamiliar and I wasn't unhappy. Or simply, I was more resilient than you. My story could be a quotable example of success that both immigrants and natives would rather hear. Yours they'd rather ignore.

For years afterward I thought I was free of you. Seeing your last name made me realize I wasn't.

WELL-LETTERED

For well over twenty-eight years I've been reading other people's letters. I don't mean reading someone else's letters or emails on the sly. I'm referring to the published letters of writers I admire. I might not have become their avid reader had it not been for the downfall of communism and the demise of censorship in the part of the world I come from. Once that happened, Polish publishers quickly responded to the public's craving for openness, honesty and truth, for books untainted by communist ideology. A slew of historical accounts and memoirs, as well as formerly banned novels and poems, appeared in print. They were soon joined by the letters of intellectuals, artists, poets and writers, which couldn't have come out prior to 1989. If my original motivation for reading published letters could be called political—after all, I did want to fill in the blanks in Polish history and literature that existed because of censorship—I soon discovered that I was granted more: I got access to the private personas of my favorite writers.

The first such book I read was the collected letters of Czesław Miłosz and Thomas Merton, which was published in Poland in 1991 (the American edition, *Striving towards Being*, appeared in 1996). Their epistolary exchange began in 1958 when Miłosz still lived in Montgeron, in France. Merton wrote to him after reading *The Captive Mind*, thus beginning a ten-year correspondence that went on until Merton's death. The two writers were true pen pals because they hadn't met in person until some years later when Miłosz was already living in the US and teaching at Berkeley.

As my love for reading published letters grew, in the next years I pored over Zbigniew Herbert's extensive correspondence: with his philosophy professor and mentor Henryk Elzenberg, with Jerzy Turowicz, the long-time editor of the Catholic weekly *Tygodnik Powszechny*, and with Miłosz, which came out in 2006, after both poets were already dead. I also read the letters Herbert exchanged with Stanisław Barańczak, the Polish poet and Slavics professor at Harvard, and more recently his correspondence with the married couple, Julia Hartwig and Artur Międzyrzecki, two poets who were his close friends. All those letters are great testimonies to friendship, even if later some friendships disintegrate, the way Miłosz and Herbert's did.

While some writers have left behind only a small stash, others have bequeathed us so many that they require multiple volumes. Virginia Woolf, a strong believer in epistolary conversation, says in *Jacob's Room* that "Life would be split asunder without letters," a sentiment many writers share. She was much impressed with the ongoing publication of Horace Walpole's letters, which in their entirety would encompass forty-two volumes. Woolf's own letters comprise six volumes, an impressive number until we compare it with George Eliot's nine. Franz Kafka was another prolific and obsessive correspondent. In 1912, between October 23 and the end of the year, he penned one hundred letters to Felice Bauer, the woman he was twice engaged to. After they broke up the second time, he destroyed her letters to him, but fortunately for his future readers he held on to his own that Felice had returned. Few writers, however, can compete with Rainer Maria Rilke or Henry James in their epistolary output: each of them wrote well over ten thousand letters. The complete edition of James's will consist of 140 volumes. At times, only a few of the writer's letters survive, which was the case with Bruno Schulz, most of whose correspondence perished in the Second World War. Yet even that remnant has added to the scanty information we possess about the author.

*

There's no question about the value of writers' correspondence for biographers or scholars, but since I'm not a scholar or a biographer, I can't explain my predilection by saying I need to engage in research. Because letters arise out of what is immediate, palpable, and local, reading writers' letters brings me as close as I can ever come to eavesdropping on the writer's everyday voice, its spontaneous cadences, without art's subterfuges, transmutations, and sublimations. I don't set out to search for clues that would enhance my interpretation of their work, although such clues emerge now and then. Writers live in their letters in a different way from how they live in their poems, essays, or novels. I'm interested in the writer's unmediated reactions to the surrounding world, in the mind at work, in the private portrait of the artist, though I'm well aware that even painters' self-portraits, which embody the gist of their self-knowledge, aren't a mirror reflection but an oblique impression that may be even the result of the artist's imagination.

Obliqueness, however, can unveil some personal truth and convey the sense of the person behind the writer. Hence letters, even at their most oblique, can let us, in the words of Henry James, "trace the implication of things." It would be naïve to expect truth and nothing but the truth in letters or, for that matter, in any kind of personal writing, including diaries ostensibly intended for their authors' eyes only. Neither private journals nor letters convey the whole raw truth of one's life. Writers know that unless they destroy their private writings or have restrictions placed on them, their letters or diaries are more than likely to appear in print one day. The accepted wisdom is that if a writer doesn't destroy them, he or she considers the possibility of publication. Sometimes overzealous family members, ignoring the writers' wishes, take matters into their own hands and forbid publication for fear that the family's reputation will be sullied. Thomas Mann burned parts of his diaries that dealt with his homosexuality. Philip Larkin's diaries, apparently on his orders, were destroyed after his death by his secretary. With an eye toward future publication, some writers take pains to create a positive image for posterity. There are also those who refuse to varnish their lives and want to create the impression that they withhold nothing and record their life in its unadorned form. In 2013 the third and last volume of Sławomir Mrożek's diaries came out in Poland, in which the well-known author of plays and short-stories in the absurdist vein engages in merciless self-analysis, as if he were dissecting an insect under a microscope. Like Kafka in his diaries, Mrożek writes with shocking honesty about his failures and frustrations, his anxieties and vulnerabilities, his obsessions and complexes. If his diary is a mirror, it's a distorting mirror that mocks and sneers but nevertheless helps him mull over pressing existential and philosophical questions.

EWA HRYNIEWICZ-YARBROUGH

In contrast Witold Gombrowicz's *Diary* is a completely literary construction meant from its very first famous words for publication ("*Monday* Me. *Tuesday* Me. *Wednesday* Me") since each segment he wrote was published in monthly installments by the Polish émigré journal *Kultura*. Gombrowicz serves the reader his carefully prepared self-portrait, donning all kinds of masks—that of a neurotic genius, a serious publicist, an iconoclast, a clown—but in doing so he discloses his contradictions, hesitations, weaknesses, and admits his desire for fame. Underneath all his posturing, there's the deeper truth of the writer's life, "the remorseless truth, between the lines," as Mark Twain said in his comment on autobiography. Paradoxically, Gombrowicz's other diary, the private and intimate *Kronos*, which came out in Poland in 2013, is a reductive bore, telling us less about its author than the one carefully constructed with the public in mind.

In the same way—no matter what the writer wants to attain—letters are an attempt to construct one's own life. Like all communications with others they often exhibit confabulations, false notes, and evasions. That aside, letters do contain spontaneous reactions to the present moment and to everyday occurrences, allowing the reader to follow the sometimes dramatic arc of the correspondence. We see it in the previously mentioned letters of Czesław Miłosz and Thomas Merton, where they discuss subjects as varied as communism, religion, popular culture, campus unrest, poetry, and the ethics of being a writer, occasionally challenging each other. At one point Miłosz critiques one of Merton's books for dealing with spiritual issues in a superficial way, but their philosophical or political disagreements don't adversely affect their epistolary friendship. In Hannah Arendt and Mary McCarthy's correspondence *Between Friends*, the two temperamentally different writers and intellectuals talk about politics, their own books and articles, and exchange gossip, Arendt more reticently, McCarthy talking freely about her emotional life and asking her friend's advice. Now and then they disagree and take issue with each other's opinions. Their letters show the day-to-day personalities of the two correspondents and their genuine responses to events, reflecting the rhythms of their private lives as well as of their times. Very often their exchanges display the intimacy of two friends talking over coffee where each topic, lofty or mundane, is interesting.

*

Considering how many writers have left us their abundant correspondence, those of us who love writers' letters aren't likely to run out of reading material. But can we hope that present-day writers will leave as rich a trove as the previous generations did? Will we have another Kafka writing letters to a modern-day Felice, the fascinating back and forth of Elizabeth Bishop and Robert Lowell, or the gracious correspondence of Eudora Welty and William Maxwell that spanned over fifty years of friendship? Will the genre of writers' letters—if it can be called a genre—be redefined, undergoing a miraculous revival and thriving, or will it be consigned to oblivion, going the way of yellow legal pads and typewriters, and turning into an anachronistic phenomenon that will have to be explained to future generations? I remind myself that a hard disc, had it existed in the past, could have preserved all those letters that were lost through individual carelessness or history's brutality, and that thanks to it some e-letters of writers may be preserved for posterity.

Some time ago I took note of the publication of *Here and Now: Letters*, the correspondence of Paul Auster and J.M. Coetzee. The added bonus was that I like the fiction of both writers. Their book, I thought, was proof that letter writing was still alive and well, and I chastised myself for being a doomsayer. *Here and Now* covers three years of the exchange, initiated by J.M. Coetzee. The first two letters discuss friendship, very appropriately, since letters help maintain and nourish it. Auster says that friendship is based on admiration, and these letters show a lot of the writers' mutual admiration. Both admit to being technophobes, so it seems only natural that they would choose snail mail. A few times Coetzee sends an email to his friend's wife asking her to print it. Eventually he begins to fax all his responses while Auster continues with old-fashioned paper letters. They cover a medley of topics—native language and translation, the state of poetry, other writers, world economy, the Middle-East, digital libraries, their "shared dismay at the way the world is going"—but the one subject that keeps recurring is sports, which both correspondents happily fall back on when they seem to have run out of things to say.

I don't know for sure, but I suspect those letters were written for immediate publication. Their writers seem models of generosity and considerateness, always on their best behavior, seeing eye to eye on everything, without even the smallest disagreement. There's not a single critical comment about a fellow writer (the one sore spot Auster acknowledges is a particular reviewer), not to mention gossip. If one were to judge on the basis of the letters alone, neither Auster nor Coetzee shares in the rest of the humanity's weaknesses and follies. Their letters show no passion, are lukewarm and short on spontaneity. Many of them are written in response to what looks like a set homework topic—"memory might be something we could investigate. Or, if that is too vast a subject, the deceptions of memory." The book is self-conscious to a fault, and if I had never read Auster's and Coetzee's novels, it wouldn't induce me to read their fiction.

Letters are always composed with a specific person in mind, intended for the eyes of him or her only, and they connote intimacy and privacy. Few writers therefore ponder the possibility of going public with them, at least not at the moment of putting marks down on paper, since instantaneous publication would undermine the fundamental premise behind such an exchange. Auster and Coetzee's letters violate the accepted scenario, and the end result bears the telltale signs of the breach: their letters read as if a censorious stranger had been peering over each writer's shoulder while he was writing. I'm not saying they should have waited until one or both of them were dead, although that seems to have been the broadly accepted norm.

Formerly, when writers wrote letters and considered their appearance in print, they mostly thought about posterity, assuming, I believe, that their novels, poems, and essays would outlive them and that later generations would want to read their letters as companion pieces to their literary work. They demonstrated the kind of confidence that writers can't have any more. Today's writers realize that the reading public is fickle and that once they're not around, absent from the media and the social media, their books will vanish from readers' memory and face obsolescence. It's better then to get what you can from those who are alive while you're alive too. Despite their frequent claims to the contrary, writers cannot repudiate their time and culture. They too exhibit its propensity for haste, instant gratification, narcissism, and the blurring of the line between the private and the public. And even though some of them dislike social media, they are like Facebook users, in their impatience for the reading public to have quick access to everything they write, including their private correspondence.

THE HOUR OF LEAD

It's two am and I'm wide awake. I haven't experienced it for almost two months, and I have begun to entertain the thought that the intruder that robs me of sleep was gone for good. It starts in the lower right side where it stabs like an ice pick and then radiates all the way to my back, leaving the point where it entered frozen and numb. I lie still, hoping to placate it, lull it into a cease-fire. I should know better, though. I've had plenty of opportunities to learn that it'll continue its forays for several hours. I shift, lie on my side, and try to breathe evenly. I want to believe that *my body* can control my body. But all my efforts are futile. This is the kind of pain that holds you in a vise, and nothing takes the edge off it. Defeated, I reach into the drawer of my bedside table and grope for a pill. After a little while I manage to fall asleep. I wake around six—or rather it wakes me up as if trying to re-assert itself, to remind me that it's still in charge. Two pills later it abates, but I sense it hovering nearby, ready to pounce on me again the moment the pill begins to wear off. Even now I can feel a discomfort in my side. Luckily, it's only an echo of the real thing.

I've had this pain for almost two years now. I can date its onset more precisely than that of other happenings in my life, whose outlines got blurry with time and which I can barely recollect. It made sure it wouldn't join the ranks of unimportant incidents buried in my memory. It left its signature in my mind, which is like those notes we scribble under dates on the calendar. The days that have something written underneath are the ones that acquire importance—the days that exist—while the blank ones blend together, sentenced to oblivion.

*

When it first started I thought it was a freak incident, one of those pranks our bodies like to play to bring us down to earth and remind us we are not just consciousness and spirit but clay and matter too. After it recurred several times, I went to see my doctor, and he ordered tests. All negative. Since there was no medical explanation, it wasn't supposed to exist. But I didn't trust the results. I knew women could be so sensitive to the signals from their bodies that they often sense something amiss before doctors can recognize it. Even though the pain was very real to me, my doctor was skeptical. For all I know he may have thought it was the product of an overwrought imagination. Then one day I hurt so badly that my husband had to take me to the emergency room where I was given morphine. The hospital ran a CAT scan. It yielded nothing. I was relieved and disappointed at the same time. No disease was lurking in my body and sending me signals about it, yet pain without reason is as difficult—or maybe even more difficult—to deal with as a specific physical problem. I was never a believer in the ability of science to explain everything but was dismayed when it was unable to give me any answers. The world's mysteries are fine, A mysterious pain is unsettling and scary.

Pains whose origins are murky and which are impossible or difficult to diagnose invariably end up being called psychosomatic. As labels go, this one tops others in vagueness and confirms how little, despite all medical advances, we know about our bodies. Doctors often resort to the term when they are unable to diagnose what the patient is suffering from. And they seem to emphasize the *psyche* part rather than the *soma* as though pain could be abstracted from the body and aggravated by the patient's volatile emotions and overall psychic makeup, particularly if the patient happens to be a woman. If the psychosomatic diagnosis was supposed to comfort me and dispel my worries, it didn't succeed. I still can't be sure that some secret disease isn't hatching somewhere and won't announce itself later. Yes, the tests have been negative, but I can't deny the existence of the pain, which may be an indication of sickness. And each episode makes me consider that possibility.

*

I can talk about dealing with pain when I'm not experiencing it. I can even promise myself that next time I'll fight it, try to master and conquer it. Deep down, though, I know these are fake metaphors which don't reflect pain's reality as much as they reflect wishful thinking. When the pain first proclaimed its presence, I was in a fighting mood. It was the enemy I wanted to eradicate, and I was sure I could. Accepting it was out of question—the whole idea smacked of martyrdom, and I wasn't ready for it. But eventually I had to do just that since being free of it is no longer part of the equation. I now consider it an unwelcome but expected and even normal part of my life.

*

When I was growing up, I convinced myself I could stand pain easily. I wasn't athletic so this may have been my way of compensating for lack of physical prowess. I never cried when I was given a shot; I held back tears when I fell and scraped my knee; I didn't even cry when the metal edge of a seesaw sliced my cheek or when my sleigh careened straight into a lamp-post. My grandmother, a tough woman who during the war years used to smuggle food into Warsaw to keep her family from starving, was visibly disturbed to see blood splattered all over my face during the latter two mishaps. My threshold for pain couldn't have been very high. I was simply too much in shock to feel anything, like a football player who in the heat of the game doesn't realize he has broken ribs.

I remember that each time I hurt myself, someone, my mother, uncle, or a neighbor, would tell me that all my aches would be gone by the time of my wedding. Other children in Poland heard the same thing. I'm not sure how those words referring to what—to a child—was light years away could have cheered up a seven- or a ten-year old, but they did. We were too young to understand their wisdom about happiness obliterating all memory of misery and grief, but we tried to be brave and not cry. We were used to having our teeth pulled and drilled with no shots to minimize discomfort, most likely because Novocain was hard to come by and anesthesia was reserved only for major surgery. I remember that when I complained I heard, "It can't be *that* bad."

The culture I lived in imparted an unambiguous message: pain is something people don't talk about. They bear it valiantly. I wonder what produced that attitude, which is no longer prevalent. Could it have been the brutality and hardship of the war, still vivid in our grandparents and parents' memories? My mother was in her early teens when the Nazis committed atrocities on the streets of Warsaw. Maybe she just couldn't bring herself to treat my aches and scrapes as anything but a minor nuisance that would soon be gone. Today's Polish children, just like their American counterparts, can cry all they want when they've been hurt, and solicitous family members fuss over them and comfort them with hugs and kisses, not with words about the pain being all gone by their wedding day. I must have learned my childhood lessons well: to this day I try to hold my tears. I learned, however, no longer to pretend that I'm not hurting when I am. I'm still wary of analgesics. I never take anything for a headache unless it's really bad, and because I hate the feeling of numbness in my face, my dentist knows he should give me very little Novocain. Even now with this inexplicable pain, I avoid pills and want to believe it will leave on its own.

*

Until recently I never had any serious bouts of sickness. When I turned sixty, things changed as they tend to when we get to be a certain age. I started to feel some minor aches, daily reminders of my aging body. This other pain, though, that assails me at night doesn't belong to that group. Luckily it comes and goes, with sometimes long breaks in between. Because I only have to cope with it for several hours at a time, I refuse to call it chronic. I don't want the label to become self-fulfilling. Pain in Polish is masculine so I always keep thinking of it as "he." The personification lets me fictionalize it, give form to its chaos. It doesn't lessen it, just as the neuter gender in English does nothing to neutralize it, but this anthropomorphic trick returns me to my native tongue and somewhat eases my mind. It makes it seem less like a monstrous spawn of some metaphysical void. I'm not the only person who resorts to linguistic trickery when dealing with pain. A poet friend of mine, who in his early twenties suffered from a particularly virulent form of rheumatoid arthritis, began to think of himself in the third person. Viewing himself as someone else allowed for distancing, which helped him cope better with his crippling affliction. It was this other person, this *he* and not the *I*, who was hurting and sick.

*

Soon I may begin to divide my life into before and after. Before the arrival of pain, I felt a seamless connection to my body and never viewed it as a separate entity. Even though grammatically speaking, I have my body, I never viewed my relationship with it in terms of ownership, and I never imagined a moment when I'd want to disown it. But now as the repository of contentment and pleasure has also become a repository of distress, when the pain is at its worst, I sometimes wish I could shuck myself out of it and free my imprisoned *I*. I don't mean it, of course, for longer than a few minutes, when the pain is at its peak. At those moments, grammar notwithstanding, my body has me, owns me completely, and the original grammatical situation doesn't hold, but is devilishly reversed.

*

I now watch for any tremor or quiver that might herald the pain's arrival. I keep hoping I'll detect what triggers it, yet I still have no clue. I only know that most of the time I can expect it at night. In the daytime other things would compete with it, but when the house is quiet and the world is asleep, it can lord it over me like a jealous lover who wants my undivided attention. When it comes, I can't hide from it, can't read or talk or even stare out the window. It shuts everything off, severs all ties, swallows the world until the whole world hurts in a meta-moment in which I'm taken out of my body and watch myself. In this perfect Zen moment space shrinks, time thickens and stops. It's all-absorbing, like love-making, always in the here and the now.

*

Pain is impossible to translate into language. A disparity between what we experience and our inability to express it becomes more conspicuous than in any other situation. Doctors and nurses use the scale from 1 to 10 when they want patients to describe the intensity of their suffering, as if the objective rationality of numbers could convey a subjective perception better than words. Numbers, though, are inadequate and reductionist, and only prove how hopelessly helpless we are in trying to capture something as commonplace as pain. My 5 will be another person's 10, and both correspond poorly to the reality of pain.

*

I used to feel something akin to an atavistic fear when faced with another's suffering. Who wants to heed the warnings about our own vulnerability and mortality? It's easier to keep pretending that it, like death, is supposed to happen to other people. Once I crossed that threshold, it stopped being an abstraction, but can I say that I'm now closer to comprehending what others may feel? There's a huge difference between my pain and the gall bladder attack my neighbor was telling me about the other day. Mine is real, hers is less so. Though sick with worry, we don't even feel the pain of loved ones. Luckily, culture and custom have taught us how to react, to say "I feel your pain" because this is the proper thing to do. We're lucky, too, that nature and instinct protect us from truly feeling it.

If we did suffer with everybody else, we wouldn't be able to live. I'm not indifferent when I say that empathy can only go so far. When I'm hurting, I'm selfish, focused on my pain, and not on the possible altruistic or transcendental value that my suffering may have.

*

Each time the pain recedes, I'm grateful that once again I've been allowed to re-join the planet of the well. During the spell I had to be with myself much more than ever before, naked and defenseless, and now I again belong with others. I feel delivered, the way I do after the plane I was on has landed safely following a turbulent flight. The world has returned, it feels new, and it waits again to be made and filled.

Will that scenario play itself out all the time? I doubt it. One day the reprieve may not arrive. Other afflictions are more than likely to join this one. I'm getting older by the day and am aware that my body will start fading. The time will come when this pain will seem minor and trifling, and the experience a mere rehearsal of what still lies in store.

MAD MÉNARDS

Translation is a labor of love. Unless one translates a classic of fiction by a long dead writer and Oprah hoists it onto the bestseller list, the way she did with Pevear and Volokhonsky's rendition of *Anna Karenina*, it rarely delivers monetary rewards. Consequently, almost no one chooses translation as a full-time career. I've always translated what I love, knowing from the start there will be little or no money in the undertaking. Once, though, I made an exception and ignored my own convictions: I translated a novel I hated. I agreed to do it because at the time we were in dire financial straits. I didn't make much, but it was more than I'd ever earned from any other project before and more than I've ever earned since. The experience was so wrenching I vowed never to sell out and always choose love over money.

Becoming fascinated with a piece of prose or poetry is therefore a prerequisite for me to embark on a translation project. When that happens, I want to make the object of my affection more mine than even the closest reading would allow. And there's no better way to possess a text than to translate it—to remove it from its natural linguistic and cultural environment and place it in a different one, kidnap it as it were, and hope it'll feel at home in its new home, like those ancient Egyptian obelisks transported to Rome, which now seem so much part of the city's architectural landscape that few residents or tourists ponder their foreignness and pagan provenance.

Since the text gives me no direct access, I have to overcome its resistance, journey inside it, reach into its hidden places, dig out its secrets, appropriate the alien space, and let a stranger inhabit my mind so I can speak in another's voice while using my own words to convey the meaning, which—uncannily—has become my own. I don't mean identification with the writer. I approach the text through my own linguistic subjectivity and life experiences. I consider myself a partner in the endeavor, not a servant of the author or the text. They both have my devotion and loyalty, but translation isn't self-abnegation. It's about self-affirmation: what I translate emerges from me. The thrill that was the writer's has now become mine, but it's a different kind of thrill as I can never duplicate the freedom of the creator. The process that was spontaneous or even subconscious for the writer has to become calculated and deliberate. I feel a thrill when I find a phrase which does justice to the original text because translation is about faithfulness—within reason, of course.

Who would dare follow in the footsteps of Pierre Ménard from the famous Borges story on the paradoxes of translation? In his mad ambition Ménard wanted to write *Don Quixote*, which would repeat the original text of Cervantes line by line and at the same time be its different reconstruction in another language. The key words here are *the same* and *different*, two propositions that can only coexist in fiction but which succinctly summarize one of the paradoxes of translation and each translator's struggle with the impossible task at hand. Translators know all too well that they practice an imperfect art which depends on what Czesław Miłosz called "the conscious acceptance of imperfect solutions." As such, it causes doubt, frustration, anxiety. Since the original is never stable, can I ever be sure of the text's meaning even if its author cannot be? Goethe famously said that the poet knows only what he wanted to write, not what he wrote.

Ultimately, though, translation is about hope. It's a promising encounter with otherness: two strangers meeting, engaging in a dialogue, becoming inseparable, even if later they have to go through the inevitable breakup when the translator is ready to share the object of her love. Unlike other partings, this one should be happy. I rejoice at the completion of my work and am eager for it to go out into the world while I retreat behind the scenes. There's a caveat here, though. To paraphrase Paul Valéry's well-known dictum: a translation is never finished; it is abandoned. I try to avoid re-reading my translations. I know all too well that I would begin to think of other alternative and possibly better versions.

Translation studies programs have made terms such as *foreignizing, exoticizing, domesticating*, and *naturalizing* part of many translators' vocabulary as if the art or craft of translation had to be legitimized by theoretical underpinnings which have little to do with the nitty-gritty practice and fail to capture the endeavor's elusive character. Most translators today subscribe to the notion that the original text's foreignness should be palpable. Like them, I don't want to replace all the foreign references with ones from the culture of the target language, but I also don't want the reader to be constantly aware that he's reading a translated text, with the translator breathing down his neck when the reader *should* be communing intimately with the author. The time comes for the writer-reader

relationship to be established to the exclusion of the translator.
There's no need for the original twosome of the writer and the
translator to metamorphose into a ménage à trois.

A NON-SENTIMENTAL JOURNEY

Each summer when I travel to Poland, I re-visit the place that was my first home. I tell myself I have to see family. But I also go to see how much there is in me of what I left behind and how much of me there is in it. I don't count on finding myself in a time warp. I hope for an encounter with my past, knowing all too well that it's impossible to enter what exists only in the subjective time of my memory. My visits can yield nothing more than crumbs, odd fragments, loose impressions, which, despite their chaotic character, feed my memory. A clothing store in one of the buildings on the town's main street makes me remember the bookstore housed in the same space when I attended elementary school. An empty area where a row of tall maples used to grow reminds me of my preschool playground that the trees gave shade to. A familiar looking stranger's face brings back the woman who lived in a small wooden house right next to the railroad crossing, surrounded by lilacs the neighborhood kids raided when the shrubs were in bloom. My mind registers these random items, yet they refuse to coalesce until I have left, as if the din of the here-and-now dissolved my past's contours and I could exist solely in the present. I need distance and solitude to sort through the recovered debris of memory and recapture what I can of my lost past. It's when I'm gone that the details, like segments of a mosaic, come together and turn into images, scenes, narratives. Being away, I can smell the smoke from fall fires and the wet odor of the soil in the fields, and conjure up in their totality the days when my school went to a collective farm to dig potatoes. I can feel the frosty air biting my cheeks when I pull my sled up the hill and keep riding it down until it gets dark, and my toes feel cold and numb in the thick woolen red and blue socks my grandmother knitted whose tops stuck out of my ungainly dark brown boots polished each Sunday morning by my father. I'll hear the neighbor from the top floor of our building yelling "Daaarek" through her kitchen window to get her son to come home for supper while all the children are playing ball in the backyard on a warm June evening, hoping for a reprieve from their own mothers. What I thus recollect seems more vivid and real than the sights I see when I visit.

We like to bemoan time's thievery and to bewail its destruction of our childhood dreams about permanence, but if the past has been plundered, a fixative has been applied to it since only things that vanish stay forever the same, immune to change, frozen in memory. How credible is my memory? I won't claim it's foolproof. I sometimes remember what I couldn't have witnessed. I'm fine with some of its failures, as long as it retains the emotional weight and meaning of experience.

*

When I left the small provincial town I grew up in, I was ready to go. The last year of high school I dreamed of escaping to the larger world the way Chekhov's three sisters dreamed of moving to Moscow. At that time, I had no conception of loss, and like a child who believes the golden summer days will last forever, I thought that even with my absence, nothing would end and my life in the town would somehow be preserved, and, when I returned, I could easily retrieve what I left behind. I always came home for the holidays, stayed in touch with friends, saw traces of my previous life everywhere. While there were changes, my frequent visits let me see them soon after they happened, so they remained in my continuous present. Eventually my ties to my hometown weakened as they invariably do.

But it was my moving away to America that began the process of disappearance. I left for the States in 1984 and returned only briefly to Poland the following summer. After that visit I stayed in the US beyond the two years that my exchange program allowed because I'd married an American. Six years later, a year after the demise of communism, I went to Poland and visited my hometown with my husband and our two daughters. By then I could safely enter the country and not worry whether I'd be permitted to leave. That trip was nostalgic, bitter sweet. I was moved to see the place where I'd grown up. I badly wanted it to be the way I remembered it, and yet I also welcomed any changes that were the harbingers of the new political order. And even though my aesthetic sense revolted against some of the ugly manifestations of the newly embraced capitalism—the disorderly open-air market on the town's outskirts selling practically everything, or the previously non-existent gaudy billboards dotting the roads—I knew they were signs of the changing times. Time alone knows how to do its job and make things disappear from the visible world, but the process would have been gentler and slower were it not for the political overhaul which contributed to the changes accelerating with each passing year.

Now the town I knew is gone, and when I visit I hear the voice whispering, You're no longer ours and we're no longer yours. You've left, you've forsaken us, so what do you expect?

Some of my old high school friends have never left and have maintained a sense of continuity. Since the town and its vicinity have changed before their eyes, they would have to see the *before* and *after* photos to realize how profound those changes have been. For them, not much has been lost of the familiar surroundings of their childhood and adolescence; they smoothly moved into adulthood and never experienced a rupture. Whereas their connection to the place remained intact, mine was loosened when I went to college and broken when I left for the United States. My loss of connection to the place entailed the loss of connection to my friends. I still see two of them when I go back, even though both they and I sense that we do it out of loyalty to our shared past since there's little we share now. When we get together and exchange the required pleasantries and basic information about our families, our conversations invariably lead to questions beginning with "Do you remember?" Like most such reminiscences, ours look pale. They remind me of stories children try to tell, skeletal summaries of what this or that someone did. They jog my memory and help me later recall some incidents in their full glory. Someone reading this might think I'm morbidly obsessed with the past. I'm not. I even wonder sometimes if I'd be going there so often if my family moved away.

*

I don't mourn the disappearance of the town I grew up in. It's still there. It's just not the town I used to live in: its tissue isn't the same. The Teutonic castle that lay in ruins has been carefully restored. Footbridges span the canal and the river outlets, so the walk to the municipal beach takes one third of the time it used to; an amphitheater has been built close to the lake where bands perform and plays are staged in the summer; a lot of old buildings have been given a face lift and boast freshly painted facades; and the barracks dating back to the Prussian garrison and later occupied by the Polish troops have been converted into high-end apartment buildings and luxury stores. All the changes are for the better. They represent the leap the country took from communism to democracy and a free market economy.

Though I still recognize the places I knew as a child, they're not what they were. I used to ride my bike on the sidewalk along Jakub Lake and by a dairy. Once past it I'd take a left on the road that had signs saying "Toruń," a university city about 130 kilometers away. I'd bike a while longer and turn left again, this time onto a dirt path in the woods. About ten minutes later I'd come to a small lake covered with water lilies, my secret refuge, peaceful and quiet. Now right across from where I used to enter the forest is a huge meat processing plant, and the formerly sleepy road is full of loud trucks and exhaust fumes. The old German cemetery in the middle of town, where each October my friends and I tidied the graves of the Germans whose families escaped before the Red Army arrived, is gone. The hospital I was born in hasn't changed much but the area around it has. It was originally located in an isolated spot that couldn't even be called the outskirts. Now apartment buildings have crept up to it, and it's surrounded by businesses and close to a heavily trafficked highway. If by some miracle I were a child again, I wouldn't be able to sled down the hill across from our apartment building. Concrete steps make the climb and the descent easy, and little stores occupy the space of the dingy apartments where the tough kids from our neighborhood lived.

*

Whenever I go to the area, I stay either with my sister or with my aunt. This time I've been staying for a few days with my aunt in Olsztyn, the city which many years ago seemed glamorous compared to my hometown. I often went there with my high school friend, Basia. We'd go to a café that served the best Napoleon pastries and, in summertime, strawberry ice-cream with large pieces of fruit, their specialty. Then we'd stop by a secondhand bookstore across the street from the café, where I bought the Polish translation of Truman Capote's *The Grass Harp*, and on a subsequent visit his *Other Voices, Other Rooms* because the owner saved it for me after someone brought it to the store. He remembered that I had told him I wanted to major in English and was trying to read any contemporary British and American writers I could lay my hands on.

My hometown is about forty kilometers west of Olsztyn. I usually travel there in a car, my sister's or my uncle's, since no one in my family lives there anymore. Today, though, I choose to go on a train, maybe trying to recreate the way I used to travel years ago. I also want to be alone. I've decided to visit the house we used to live in. My motivation is scientific, if you will. I want to see what it looks like. The apartment building has been there all along, yet not once during my many visits did I feel like going there. Was it my last sentimental outpost where old memories could stay sealed without having to be subjected to the corrective of reality?

*

You can enter and exit the station on both sides of the tracks, but I exit the way I used to, not through the main building since we lived on the opposite side. The house across the street is still there, looking better than it once did. I walk alongside a concrete fence that separates the railway tracks from the street. Lightly traveled in the past, it's congested now. Our old apartment building is a short distance away. The empty area where I used to play with neighborhood kids has been built up.

A few minutes later I reach the building. Someone has left the front door slightly ajar. I enter and climb the stairs to the third floor, counting the steps like I used to when I was a child. I stop before the door to our old apartment and listen. It's silent. The whole building is quiet in a way it never was when I lived there. It couldn't have been with twenty-eight children of different ages living within its walls, from infants to teenagers, the result of the postwar baby boom. It was a very communal place back then—neighbors stopping by to chat or borrow sugar, children running up and down, doors opening and shutting, noise and havoc. The interior has a smell I can't recognize; it's not the smells of cooking coming from all the apartments and mingling together the way they used to. If someone is cooking the smells don't escape outside. I'd like to sit on the stairs as I once did, waiting for my mother to come home or for my grandmother to return from the bakery. These are the stairs my father climbed lugging buckets of coal from the cellar, the steps I used to skip two at a time when in a hurry to announce some momentous news to my grandmother peeling potatoes in the kitchen. I touch the banister I tried to slide down after I saw our neighbor's son doing it. But it's not the same banister. And the girl sliding is and isn't me. Maybe I would feel more like her extension if I hadn't left. She is now a shadowy figure whom I have a hard time recognizing just as I can't recognize the building I once lived in.

The seams between the past and the present haven't come unstitched. If I expected an epiphany, it hasn't arrived. This visit has confirmed what I already sensed—that as we try to resurrect the past, memories alienate us from ourselves. We begin to see our former selves as strangers who might as well be fictional figures we can endow with lives that haven't been exactly, or truly, our own.

LITTLE BOWLS OF COLORS

Many languages use some form of the word "mother" to refer to a person's first language—*la lengua materna, la langue maternelle, die Muttersprache*—and rightly so. The first language we learn is generally the one our mothers speak. This may not be so obvious in monolingual families, in which both parents use the same language, but if each parent speaks a different one, the children in most cases will first speak the mother's. The words *mother tongue* suggest that the relationship we have with the first language mirrors the mysterious alchemy of our maternal relationships. Just as the mother is our entry into the world and our first love, the person from whom we learn first meanings, the beacon and the guide, so is the language with which we first make sense of the world. There's something almost supernatural in the way our mother tongue holds us in its grip. We're usually unaware of its power unless we emigrate to another country. When that happens, we begin to miss its homey warmth and yearn for its recognizable rhythms and cadences.

We never know another language the way we know our mother tongue. We know it without knowing how we know it. With a foreign language, we have to see its skeleton, its hidden machinery, all those facets that most native speakers can ignore. It takes a long time before the letters or the sounds automatically conjure up the object the way they do in the native tongue. A mother tongue exists inside us with a completeness impossible to replicate in another language; it has its roots in our whole being. Canadian researchers have recently confirmed what previously was only intuitively grasped: people who leave the country of their birth in infancy and have no memories of the language they were born into retain the pathways of the first language in their brains. These findings prove how deeply ingrained in us the mother tongue is. The brain continues to remember what by other measures has been lost. The first language is also the one that Alzheimer's sufferers lose last. A friend's father, a professor of Romance languages, fluent in French, Italian, and Romanian, lost the ability to communicate in his acquired languages long before the disease began to rob him of his mother tongue.

Polish, my first language, was our daughters' primary language, too, and they used it with each other and with me. In our home in California, my husband and I communicated in English, which they understood but spoke only when needed. But the typical scenario didn't play itself out in their case. After they entered kindergarten, the public language of school and the outside world took over. Polish was gradually relegated to bedtime storytelling and reading, and to intimate and private moments between them and me. Today they treat it as their mother's language while recognizing that English is their mother tongue. Our daughters never experienced linguistic displacement, so the shift from one language to the other happened painlessly and naturally. They still speak Polish, but with none of the ease, fluency, or versatility of their English. If they ever live in a foreign country, they will only long for English.

*

I started learning English in 1967, my freshman year of high school. I wonder if I would have developed a passion for it if it hadn't been for my teacher, Mrs. B. She'd just earned an MA in English from the University of Warsaw and moved to our town in the Mazurian Lake region. Young, attractive, well-dressed, she stuck out among the older teachers. On the first day of school, she wore a pale green twinset, a pencil skirt, and high heels, the embodiment of elegance and poise. She had several other pastel-colored button-down sweaters, which we all thought must have come from England. Against the drab and gray background, she seemed like an exotic and colorful bird, bringing in a whiff of worldliness and culture. By the time we entered high school, we had already studied Russian for four years, but most of us hated it. With English, it was love at first sight. I immediately decided I would learn to speak it well. Before long I discovered that it came to me relatively easily, and in no time I was Mrs. B's best student.

I had no plans to major in English; I wanted to be a psychologist. But midway through my junior year in high school, I changed my mind. It may have been that I became more aware aesthetically and politically. Just as Mrs. B. personified the grace and refinement I aspired to, English turned for me into a symbol of everything that was missing in the reality of communist Poland. It promised an escape from the constraints of a provincial environment into the larger world that I knew existed out there. It also presented a chance to transcend my daily life—to sublimate it as it were. Once I decided to study English at the university, I bought a thick notebook in which I began to jot down words to memorize. When Jorge Luis Borges writes about studying a language, he makes a comment that sums up my own experience: "Each word stood out as though it had been carved, as though it were a talisman." I learned each word separately, marveling at its beguiling strangeness and hoping it would take root in my mind. Thanks to this approach, I was never confused by the idiosyncrasies of English spelling. But even though I'm a good speller, to this day I have a hard time writing down proper names someone else is spelling out loud for me. My brain just never made room for the sounding of the English alphabet.

I was admitted to the English Department at Wrocław University after passing the entrance exams. All our classes were taught in English. We struggled trying to follow the lives of Pip and Rebecca Sharp or the complicated plot of *The Importance of Being Earnest*, but gradually novels, plays, and even poems rewarded our efforts. I remember traveling home for Christmas my freshman year and laughing at some of the hilarious adventures of Mr. Pickwick, while other passengers in the compartment gave me funny looks. At that moment, I knew I was enjoying Charles Dickens the way I enjoyed books in Polish. Now and then I had to use a dictionary, but that only slowed me down and didn't detract from my delight.

When I got my MA, I could speak, read, and write in English at the level required for my teaching job. English belonged to my professional life and gave me private pleasure when I read. At that time, I had no inkling that several years later I would move to America and use this foreign language daily. In Poland, I was used to having names for everything, being able to find words in any situation, from small talk to conversations about ideas, expressing my thoughts naturally and easily. Suddenly language was no longer a reliable anchor.

I wasn't just troubled by "the paucity of domestic diction" for taking "the shortest road between warehouse and shop" that Vladimir Nabokov talks about. I had to re-draft my conceptual map, re-learn and re-experience the world through and in my new language.

*

As I experienced important life events and crossed many watersheds here, I began to develop a voice in English. You can't live in a foreign linguistic environment and not be affected by it. After some time even those who try to resist the intrusion, for fear it would contaminate the purity of their native tongue, will discover that they haven't remained outside its sphere of influence. Its tide begins to envelop you, its strains and patterns seeping into your conscious and unconscious mind. The Polish poet Zbigniew Herbert said in an interview that when he lived in a foreign country, inspiration came to him from that country's language, and he subsequently had great difficulty writing in Polish. He didn't know the language well enough to try to write in it, but the possibility fascinated him. Engendering different perceptions and thought, another language can give us a powerful mental boost.

Writers who work in a language other than their mother tongue often feel the need to analyze their choice, dissecting it from many angles, mulling it over in private, and sometimes even offering public explanations. No matter what motivated them, geopolitics or personal history, they harbor misgivings—at least at first—about the unnaturalness of their decision. Writing, after all, arises out of our most intimate core. And what can be more intimate than our internal relationship to the language which exists in the deep parts of our psyche and is ours by birth? In his essay "To Please a Shadow," Joseph Brodsky writes that "when a writer resorts to a language other than his mother tongue, he does so either out of necessity, like Conrad, or because of burning ambition, like Nabokov, or for the sake of greater estrangement, like Beckett." Of the three reasons Brodsky gives, it's the estrangement that I find most interesting. One may seek it intentionally the way Beckett did, but most often it arrives as an unexpected gift.

Some years ago at a translation seminar sponsored by Boston University, I heard Rosanna Warren say that she urges the young poets in her classes to treat English as if it were a foreign language. She wanted to warn them against the clichés that so readily spring to mind and hinder original thinking as well as to emphasize the importance of scrutinizing the linguistic boundaries within which native speakers function. Since English isn't my first language, I have no choice but to follow that directive. Estrangement makes me more attentive and cautious, with none of the flippancy people often exhibit in their mother tongue. Joseph Conrad, the writer whose example is invariably quoted in such discussions, saw himself as "a coal miner in his pit quarrying all [his] sentences out of a black night." I'm not saying that only foreigners have that experience—writing is demanding and grueling, and all writers treat language with awe and reverence—but foreigners don't have to be reminded of that. Estrangement is part of their normal interaction with their new language. They're acutely aware of its perplexities and never take it for granted. When I write in English, language moves to the forefront, the words coming from outside, as if they only were the source of meaning. I obsess about words, want to know their etymologies, pay attention to their strange provenances, and test where and how far I can go with them.

Another language may expose our linguistic inadequacies and vulnerabilities, but it can also serve as a protective screen. Dubravka Ugrešić, a Croatian novelist and essayist, is convinced that it's easier to express pain in a language that isn't ours. If while living in our native language we experienced traumatic events, we are likely to relive the pain while writing about them in it. The nonnative language, on the other hand, will cause us less pain, create emotional distance, and allow for the indispensable aesthetic detachment. And when there's no visceral, bodily connection to another language, we can become more daring and say what we would have never said in our mother tongue.

Something like that happened to me: English helped me open up. It's true that American society has fewer taboos, but it's the language which gave me the freedom I didn't feel I had in my mother tongue. We may not think about it, but we live much more in a language than in a country. The Polish poet Ryszard Krynicki says in his poem "The Effect of Estrangement" that he prefers to read his poems in a foreign language, since then he feels less the shamelessness of his confession. Broaching certain topics in Polish would have made me feel awkward if not ashamed; in English, it was similar to whispering my sins through a wooden lattice in the confessional. I knew the priest was there, but he didn't see me and I couldn't quite see him. My sense of privacy has changed, but not to the "tell all" extent. I simply began to feel that I can share things about myself and my life, and assume that my experience is worth talking or even writing about.

I grew up knowing you weren't supposed to reveal information about your family to strangers. But this secretiveness wasn't just related to political issues, something expected in a totalitarian state. Within our own family, people tended to sidestep fraught personal subjects. As a child, I was aware of things unsaid and of the silence that followed an inconvenient question. The message my family sent me overlapped with the message of society at large, where it was understood and accepted that family members' misdemeanors—sexual transgressions, alcoholism—had to be covered up. Abuse was never discussed; neither was depression or cancer, as if silence would work its magic and make any problem go away. You weren't supposed to dwell too much on yourself or mention your successes, because this was interpreted as bragging. If someone brought up some accomplishment of yours, the correct response was to play it down. By the time you finished elementary school, you had absorbed all the dos and don'ts, and knew better than to divulge your feelings. Talking about books, films, and ideas was fine because it could be done at arm's length. And if your innate temperament tended toward introversion, as mine did, the general standards surrounding privacy could turn you into an even more reticent person whose articulateness could reveal itself only in certain subjects.

When I met my American husband, I was stunned by how freely he talked about his family life, about his father's manic-depressive episodes, his grandmother's stinginess, and about himself—his feelings, disappointments, dreams. He seemed to have no secrets while I harbored many. With English giving me protective camouflage, I gradually ventured out into the open. For a while it seemed that the person speaking wasn't exactly me and that I was playing someone else's part. In time, though, I became comfortable in this new persona. I could talk frankly about things that until then had been off limits: my grandfather's alcoholism and sexual indiscretions, my mother's emotional remoteness, my failed first marriage. I stopped bottling up my feelings, frustrations, anxieties. I'm not saying that I'm no longer reserved, only that my second language has helped me overcome some of my past reticence. That change has also affected the way I communicate with others in my mother tongue. I now share with them what I kept out of view before and tell things my American friends already know about me.

But English helped me get unlocked in more ways than one. Though in high school I toyed with the idea of becoming a writer, I don't believe I would have begun writing if I had continued living in Poland. It's as if dislocation combined with a new language had freed my creative muse. I began translating—at first into English—and a while later I tried my hand at writing. After the initial period, when I felt as though I were trying to play a four-hand piano piece with two hands, writing in English began to feel as natural to me as writing in Polish had been.

As much as I don't like the word *reinvent*—it smacks too much of self-help manuals—my second language did re-invent me. If the idea of personal transformation is very American, then in the process I have assimilated some of the cultural gospel of my adopted country. The change I underwent was prompted by the change in my external circumstances, but the outward conditions ultimately led me to who I may have been all along. By peeling off the inauthentic layers in myself, I may have reached the hidden core of my innate disposition.

English has also transformed my relationship with my mother tongue which I have left but not abandoned or betrayed. Thanks to English, I'm more aware and appreciative of Polish. I can go into raptures about its flexibility, about its almost endless possibilities of creating diminutive and augmentative forms, and about the ease of coining new words. In my role as a translator, I avail myself of and rejoice in its resources—the prefixes, suffixes, declensions and conjugations, gender-marked endings, perfect and imperfect tenses, all of which allow for prodigious inventiveness and creativity.

If Facebook had a question about our relationship with languages, my answer could only be: it's complicated. My two languages have forged a singular alliance. They live parallel and independent existences. For many years, I was in the habit of instantaneously translating from English into Polish in my head, or the other way round, often asking myself how I would say this or that in the other language. I stopped doing that when I realized that one language no longer needed to be bolstered by the other. Now I try to keep them in harmony, not let them clash and contend for position. To keep both happy, I alternate my reading: a book in Polish usually follows one in English. I've noticed, too, that my internal conversations are often bi-lingual, shifting from one language to the other for no apparent reason.

*

The Polish poet Czesław Miłosz lived in America for well over thirty years, yet with the exception of a few prose pieces, he consistently wrote in Polish. He believed that changing our language meant we had changed or wanted to change our identity, which to him equaled betrayal on two counts. After the political transformations in the former Eastern bloc countries, the word *immigration* has lost some of the meaning it had at the time Miłosz arrived here. I use it for lack of a better term but see it more broadly as the desire to cross borders, a desire often motivated by the longing for change. Ideally, this results in the expansion of consciousness, not the loss of identity and language. Although I left Poland, I haven't *really* left, just as when I leave the United States, I'm still here. In the age of the Internet, this is the experience of many people who live at the intersection of two languages and cultures.

These days, each time I reread Miłosz's "My Faithful Mother Tongue," where he writes "I will continue to set before you little bowls of colors/ bright and pure if possible," I'm reminded that I must prepare my own bowls of colors. But unlike the great poet, I set mine before two languages: my mother tongue and another.

Ewa Hryniewicz-Yarbrough is a native of Poland. Her essays were published in journals such as *Agni, Ploughshares, The American Scholar, The Threepenny Review,* and *TriQuarterly.* One of her pieces, "Objects of Affection" was selected for inclusion in *The Best American Essays 2012*; four others were listed among Notable Essays for 2011, 2013, 2014, 2015, and 2017. She divides her time between Boston and Kraków.

CPSIA information can be obtained
at www.ICGtesting.com
Printed in the USA
FFOW04n0700200218
45089291-45489FF

9 780998 966755